AF430961

CONTENTS

PART ONE

INTRODUCTION

*Welcome To The Meal
Of Our Lives*

The purpose of this book is to open you to the wonderful enjoyment of looking at life innovatively with all the personality types we find ourselves surrounded with.This small manual will hopefully provide a method of experiencing individuals, using a sense of humor first and most importantly, then secondly providing tools that actually allow us to benefit from our interactions. We may for the first time feel the ability to navigate through the many human encounters enjoying them, or at the very least coming through unscathed.

We will also be shown how to determine what type of food course each one of us actually represents. Surprisingly, the majority of the time, we are not the course we may at first thought.

One important point to note is this. No course is of greater value than another! Like a beautiful three course meal, we are meant to enhance each other! We are meant to complement each other in every way! This concept will be examined more closely to observe its relevance in all human relationships, ranging from the workplace to the bedroom.

Expanding this exploration even further, we will discover the dynamics of this theory reaching into the geography of even the planet itself! Interesting? Right! Read on!

CHAPTER ONE

What Is The Meal Of Our Lives

Have you ever analyzed what makes you tick? What common threads seem to hold your life together? How would you describe the daily rhythm of your life? Upon close inspection it becomes evident that certain behaviors are clues to the pattern of our lives. You will be observing these very tendencies to unravel the qualities which determine your course type.

When do you actually feel "the perfect fit?" What stimulates you? What relaxes you, enveloping you in a feeling of contentment and fulfillment?

We will be exploring these aspects for ourselves and those around us. Self knowledge is the starting point for our gourmet journey. Each course will be discussed in detail, hopefully enabling us to realize our own qualities, then progressing toward individuals we encounter, even the world itself!

An exquisitely prepared banquet is a feast for

the eyes as well as the palate. Life can be equally such a feast! Truly well developed taste buds embrace excellent cuisine, likewise, my hope is that this concept will enhance our feast of life more fully in all its aspects!

CHAPTER TWO

Appetizers

There is a reason in gourmet dining that we have a beginning course. Why is that, we may ask ourselves? First, to tantalize our sensory experience. What exactly is meant by that? A sensory experience evokes our sense of sight, smell, and texture. Secondly, and more specifically in this case, to excite our taste buds allowing them to openly embrace and anticipate what awaits us further into the meal.

One of the unfortunate practices infringing upon our eating habits, particularly in the U.S. is skipping the first course in an attempt to curb calories. Actually, if the French really do stay slim it's because they do not subscribe to this belief. I have heard it said a true gourmet needs only a bite or two to experience the intoxicating taste of the food. Unfortunately, we in America think in terms of quantity rather than quality. This is partially explained by our work ethic, such as fast food eaten at our desk, or skipping lunch entirely.

This is a practice almost unheard of in European countries. Notice, I did not include England because culturally we have that in common. Are we in the United States really that more productive? One could say we are less because we suffer more burnout due to stress. What does all of this have to do with comparing people and places? Quite a lot, actually, since an individual's eating habits are expressions of the way he/she lives life. My belief however, is we actually belong to one of the courses initially and remain so for the duration of our lives. This knowledge and awareness celebrates the banquet of humanity.

Now, there are many types of appetizers making it a bit confusing. Have you ever wondered why, in a set of circumstances with certain friends or acquaintances you felt bored or ever irritated? I know I certainly have! We may ask ourselves "what's wrong with me" or "what's going on with them?" Have you ever tried to make a meal simply opting for only a first course, thinking I'm not really that hungry, or I need to watch how much I'm spending?" How do we feel after eating, perhaps unsatisfied at best, or experiencing even a slight case of indigestion?"

How about that man or woman in your circle of acquaintances who brightens the room when they enter? They are fun, even enchanting but, have you been missing a sustaining quality in your interactions with these individuals? Now, I'm not suggesting we avoid exciting, stimulating appetizer types. They are the life of the party, we can be thankful for their presence. They are enhanced however, by the varied personalities surrounding them. Have you ever experienced the same identical group minus these people? The feeling is flat, all stimulus gone! Ah, how valuable these starter personalities really are!

Now, returning to our meal, to be more specific so many foods can begin our gourmet feast. The range runs the gamut from the subtle to the flamboyant. Let's begin simply with raw veggies and dip, light and refreshing with a little zing. What type does that remind you of? The bright, usually intelligent one who breezes in, literally a breath of fresh air. Now, if this individual is in a group of like beings you may feel like shutting the window to escape too much of this energy.

Many times a spicy substance is offered to start a meal, it can even be breaded for more impact. This is symbolic of the exciting, stimulating person who can literally take over a room. The first reaction is practically hero worship but, then exhaustion threatens because there is no buffer, just too much excitement.

Then there is the soup type. Now this type can easily be confused with the main course. You will later discover why. It's vital you experience only a cup of soup or you will not enjoy your main course. Here's why. This personality exhibits some soothing comfort but is not meant to provide the sustenance of the main course. We can celebrate these appetizer individuals in their many forms, who bring such refreshing, stimulating and tantalizing qualities to our lives. Now, bring on the main course.

CHAPTER THREE

The Main Course

We can compare the main course in many ways to the career in our lives, or the work enabling us to pay our bills. It can occupy the primary focus of our attention, but should it? This is the question we may choose to ask ourselves. Just as this part of the meal can dominate our dining experience, it is meant to be only a portion of the dining experience. If we permit this course to overpower the meal, we may feel an imbalance. Our occupation is merely an aspect of our lives. When we allow our work to identify us, it creates a lack of flow in our daily existence. How can we find success and satisfaction in our work endeavors while meeting our obligations, thereby enjoying economic freedom? Ah! That's the challenge isn't it? Our lifestyle, like our eating habits, can bring nourishment to ourselves, be fulfilling and sustaining or generate discomfort from excessive indulgence.

Now, let's talk about the people in our lives who personify the central course in our meal. There are a myriad of types who fit this category. The most obvious are those individuals who come on strong and powerful. There is no mistaking their role in life. They have definite opinions, having little hesitation stating them. Consistency is another trait easily identified with few mood swings. Many leaders in our society gain followers by exhibiting these qualities. The main course follows the appetizer in our meal, how does this work with people? Reflect upon a keynote speaker featured in an event, he/she is preceded by a rousing introduction setting the tone for the strong delivery.

The pendulum swings a bit however, in the wide spectrum of ways these types operate. The obvious bold straight forward energies resemble the meat and potatoes course. The type of meat or seafood may vary, but the presentation is very similar. Another choice on the menu for the principal course may be a sautéed or fried meat even a vegetarian dish, we don't want to leave these people out. Such selections are less distinct in both visual and taste qualities, achieving a unique identity but less in your face about it. The corresponding personality, also makes a more subtle energetic impact, but is not to be taken lightly. The digestive implications can be similar in strength as the meat and potatoes dish, it just rather sneaks up on you. Likewise, these individuals, as well, can be very significant and need to be respected as such.

Lastly, sometimes we may select a hearty stew or a full bodied soup, which offers us yet another comparison. These people are easier to take and can be very fulfilling, but the effects are shorter lived.

So, what shall we do with these foods - people? Enjoy them! Each and every one of them! They are all wonderful, but be wise, partake according to the appetizer you selected. For instance, if you ordered a light airy starter food, such as a salad, practically any of the above main courses are compatible. Be mindful of the quantity you consume, savoring each bite is very important. If your initial choice was to begin with something more zesty and provocative to your taste buds, be more gentle in the selection of your next course, such as a creamy food. If you went for a crispy, crunchy tidbit, a wise follow up may be a stew or dinner soup.

These menu references are merely suggestions. They do have a correlation to the people who fit this mold. The usual assumption is that the main course types of people are more desirable than the individuals who fit the description of appetizers and desserts. Nothing could be further from the truth. This central part of our meal is meant to be enjoyed for its attributes of strength and sustainability. Just as the people who display comparative traits can be a wonderful asset to our wellbeing, too much can cause indigestion!

CHAPTER FOUR

The Desert

How we anticipate this last course! Our meal, the tantalizing beginning, sustaining main course, and now the grand finale! The people who fit this description are quite interesting indeed! The variety of ingredients in this food category that are made into these delectable treats are equally expressed by the assortment of personalities of those we have in our lives, who are indeed our desserts. The choices seem quiet infinite, from the gentle creams to the tarts and pies, extending even to the flaming presentations. The delectable dipping chocolate fondue, cakes and fruit syrups are included in this array. WOW!

Let's begin our comparisons. The gentle soul, who leaves a sweet, soothing imprint on our lives, is quite like gelato. Following close in this category are those who are a bit like a creme brûlée, brittle on the surface , but so easy to take underneath. It just takes a tap to break through. It is definitely worth the effort to experience the succulent inner goodness. Sound like anyone you know?

The comforting aroma of the fruit tart or pie, maybe with a dollop of ice cream to top it off, is reminiscent of that individual who is always there with a sustaining word or act of kindness.

Chocolate cake carries its own energy as does its counterpart in our lives. An addictive substance in the ability to uplift our moods, truly fun! Do we know anyone like this? We must however, indulge in moderation, otherwise our enjoyment is diminished.

Most dramatically, we have the flaming presentations with the soul warming brandy flaring our nostrils! We always remember our experiences with these like minded souls. How they add sparkle and drama to our lives!

CHAPTER FIVE

What course are we?

That is the loaded question! Let's look at how we live our lives. What choices do we make, sometimes repeatedly? Therein lies the answers! Do we feel in charge of our lives or that our life is living us? What about our energy output? These are very important guidelines for consideration. Is our energy constantly being zapped? Do we feel the need to take action with issues staring us in the face? Do we long to experience a completeness, but seem lost or confused in the tidal wave of life? If any of these situations ring a bell for us, there is a strong chance we are starters, or appetizers. The very word "starters" is a strong clue! Now, I want to be very clear when I repeat, no course is superior to another. Remember the complete banquet picture.

Appetizers are rather easily pinpointed by their energetic beginnings. Where would we be without getting off to a good start? However, follow up can be sketchy, fireworks are short lived but loved in the moment! All is not lost. It is said the secret of accomplishing anything is in the assessment of the situation and the subsequent delegation of tasks. Those who find themselves fitting this description merely need to acquire main courses and desserts to complete their qualities.

This is actually what we do consciously or unconsciously. Most often we choose a partner who is very different from ourselves. This is no accident for them or us. The question is how do we handle these differences? Embrace them! Celebrate them! They are vital for us and those we choose to be with us.

Let's demonstrate how the main course and dessert round out the picture for the starters. For openers, mind the pun, the main course was not designed to get the ball rolling. It was ordained to keep the ball rolling, perhaps increase the speed of momentum. This provides the first course to take a much needed breath and sit back for a moment. Dessert types are designed to bring the works in progress to a delightful finale.These are not the primary tasks of the beginners. Now, some people may say," well, I can do all three!" My answer is yes, that may be possible, but is that the grand design, or is perhaps more pleasant to have help saving the world? Why try to do it alone?

Those of you who fit this opening category, rejoice! The world needs you, actually desperately! But, we need you to use your gifts wisely, allow others to pick up the slack to avoid burnout. Above all, be aware of how others differences just enhance you as you set the stage for taste treats to come.

CHAPTER SIX

How do I Fit?

Now that we have a pretty good idea which course we are, how do we incorporate that knowledge into our daily lives? When we looked closely what qualities typified the different food groups to determine our specific traits, we were given an overview.

Now, let's get down to the nitty gritties so to speak. Alright, say we are an appetizer and the boss is a main course. Actually, this is a very good combination! Why? Because you (appetizer) stimulate the main course. This translates to mean bringing fresh ideas to the table and inspiring the boss to implement these very ideas with enthusiasm! Thus, the manager or owner, can sustain and maintain the business actions allowing the starter to relax a little. But, problems can arise if the appetizer oversteps his/her boundaries and carries on to the next level. This is the arena of the main course or boss. The question may arise, "what if my boss doesn't seem qualified to take the necessary actions?" One of two consequences is likely to occur.

First, action will be given for the next aspect to the starter. This leaves the boss's authority intact because she/he is making the decision even though the power of action is being delegated. Secondly, the incompetence of higher management will be brought to task and changes made at that level.

Let's assume all goes well and the task at hand is brought to fruition by the first two courses. The dessert brings the sweet taste of completion for all involved. Sweet success!

Now, we have captured the optimal situation, when everyone operates in the ideal sequential order. Unfortunately, this does not always happen. Why not? When identical courses try to work in achieving the same goal, what usually occurs is the classic power struggle. Now, here's where this info comes in handy. Do we have to leave this work situation because it spells disaster? It can spell disaster, yes, but no we do not have to run, in fact it's best not to.

Say, for example, two appetizers are on different rungs of the corporate ladder, or even in a less structured situation say a committee. One is in charge and one is a worker bee. Remember, there are many types of starters, the veggies verses the jalapeño poppers for example. Each will exercise their muscles for getting the project off the ground, but each in their own way, literally with their own flavor! This is how the drama can be embraced, if we have awareness of the strategy involved.

The situation can become even more heated if

those involved are both main courses. The reason differs from the first course people. As we stated, the first course's focus is getting things going, the challenge is sustainability. The main course people are grounded and strong. These qualities are valuable to carry the project into the next phase, but a power struggle is a possibility. How can this be avoided? Remember, the succulent qualities of this main course, this delicious part of the meal, almost infinitely varied from stews, meats, seafood and nutritious veggies. They can work together provided the seasonings are compatible. Seasonings can vary considerably. Herein, lies the secret! Adjust the modes of action when interacting with two of this course type. This can be accomplished with minimal effort if you have the foresight and take the necessary actions. This will ensure compatibility with no indigestion, a parable to situations in life. To be more specific, detailed roles must be given to each main course that are responsible and substantial but not competitive.

The next and final aspect of our experience is what happens when two dessert type persons end up attempting to work together. If they are in equal positions, the main issue could be nothing gets done, but much is discussed. Why, you may ask as you follow our meal sequence? Isn't the dessert the finale? Yes, but only when the task to be completed rests on a solid foundation, which is the central or previous course. Are you following me? The picture is this - we have two people representing completion, but of what? This situation varies only slightly if one party is in a more authoritative position. The goal is to firmly establish the project at hand, only then can it be wrapped up as they say. As the job to be finished has infinitesimal variants, so likewise are the desserts designed to accomplish this. Now, let's allow ourselves to imagine the luscious array of desserts. Most of us have preferences, rather like the people we choose to enjoy. Some like cakes, others - pies or tarts, or even light fluffy pastries. Delicious puddings and custards captivate the taste buds as well. All is not lost when two desserts are thrown together, in fact, most are a combination of each other. Who doesn't love a dollop of creme on their custard, pie a la mode, and what would cake be without icing? Now, in the case of getting the work completed, if it has been firmly digested or established in the previous course of action, the finale of the desserts should be sweet and lasting. Perfect - Right!

CHAPTER SEVEN

This chapter is so vital we will be dividing it into three parts.

Relationships - Appetizers

We will begin, as always with the first course. Remember that this type is always energetic, tantalizing and gets attention! Now, here is where it gets interesting. Almost, without fail, the starters attract into their lives either main courses or desserts - very seldom do they pair up with other starters. Why? The answer is quite simple. Energetically both would burn out, having no way to recharge or nourish themselves. Humanity seeks to preserve or nourish itself, consciously or unconsciously. Platonic, heterosexual or homosexual relationships all fall into this pattern. Balance is sought, but this is not always the case. Often what happens is a drain, experienced by the other types or courses as we will illustrate. How, precisely does this play out? In friendships, appetizers are providing a refreshing change of pace for the main courses or desserts. The main course people can be a bit too substantial or heavy energetically. Along comes the zing of the appetizer and off we go, usually a mile a minute. Then comes the crash or let down. The problem can be a minor one if personal contact remains seldom and of short duration. If the time spent together becomes more lengthy and frequent the flame starts to become more intense. Romantic relationships dramatically illustrate the escalation of this energy. The starter begins to demand more and more from the main courses or desserts, whatever the combo is. The resulting occurrence is usually one of two actions. One, the main course or dessert is so drained he/she cannot keep up, the output is physically exhausted and sets boundaries, or ends the contact.

There is a more constructive alternative the appetizer person can utilize. How is this accomplished? Most intense starter types gravitate to a physical sport, or working out in a gym, maybe even something as simply soothing as a walk in nature. A creative hobby can also feed the soul and the emotions. The important quality to seek is a source of security and a feeling of being grounded. How can we know what makes us feel stronger? What types of activities or qualities do we want to feel? What inner workings do we admire in the other two courses and seek to capture for ourselves? These are clues to consider. When we discover our own magic by balancing ourselves , we can enjoy others without being an emotional bloodsucker.

Relationships - The Main Course

The principal challenge main course people experience is the thought that they are able to do it all. While, it is true that due to the fact they are energetically substantial, they do possess a form of endurance not found in the other two types, namely the appetizer and the dessert. The issue however, is one of patience. It can be a difficulty for the main course to "go with the flow" as we say. Now it's true, they are very proactive, but when control issues arise with this personality difficulties may occur. Judgements can rear their ugly heads.

What to do when we realize that's our type? This is the question. Let's dive in and search for answers.

When a main course is paired with a starter - which incidentally often occurs - here's a plan. Why are these two often a duo? Because they are a match made in heaven, as they say! The mutual attraction lies in the fact the proverbial fire of the appetizer ignites the steady strong heat of the main course, thus appeasing both energies. The dance however, must allow each course the space to perform their respective actions without stifling the other. Later in this book, we will undertake a journey showing specific situations to further illustrate these scenarios.

Simply stated, the appetizer must be allowed to exert his/her purpose of inspiration and stimulation adhering to the boundaries so vital for each. The starter must be allowed to shine their light, yet resisting the temptation to overwhelm the principle course. This action is counterproductive, to say the least, if not infuriating to the principle course. This course (main) would do well to appreciate the appetizer, yet holding the line, remaining in the comfort zone.

When two main courses get together the real challenge can present itself. We then have two energies vying for the same role! As we have noted, regarding foods there are many types of main courses. How this translates is that those in this category would profit by analyzing the qualities within themselves that would complement the other main courses in their company. Referring to the comparison of foods, one example would be potatoes accompanying the meat, fish or veggie protein part of this course. Varied types of dishes, too numerous to mention, also may enhance this main course due to their own unique properties. Individual people can follow suit by combining their strengths.

Now, what are the dynamics of the main course and dessert combo? Actually, this can be an easier flow if certain awarenesses are realized. The purpose of the dessert is to bring a pleasing completion to the meal. The same purpose is true in life - a sweet finish, whether an evening with friends, a moment of romance, or a business contact. The closure can last a moment or an evening depending on the situation. The problem happens when the main course thinks the dessert is not needed. In life situations this translates into not letting go of the final say - control issues again, or expecting the dessert to always be the grand finale! This results in excess expectations. The desired reaction would be to partake of all the final course has to offer, enjoy and savor, but realize there will be another meal!

Relationships - Ahhh The Dessert

Remember the main course may think they run the show, when in fact the dessert is very vital and at times the most memorable part of the meal, the proverbial frosting on the cake. How is this accomplished? Visualize a scrumptious meal. How is the dessert served - with a flourish! Where people are concerned, dessert types seem self-effacing, even humble, yet they yearn for their moment of recognition. In the sequence of the meal, the preparation for the final course is the clearing of all remnants of the previous courses and then the dessert is served. In life, as well it is beneficial to allow this personality (the dessert) their own space. In relationships this means we let go and take a breath. Let the closing act take place without any input from other course energies. To our surprise the dessert person can most often accomplish this finale beautifully! The secret lies in the letting go in this case of the main course. The dessert is free then, to take center stage and shine!

In the business or professional arena, this dynamic takes a slightly different twist. The dessert is perfect for literally wrapping up the loose ends of the course of action laid out by the main course go-getters. These closers are extremely valuable to the business and professional worlds. It is essential that they be allowed to accomplish their "wrapping up" unhampered by main course individuals! This is their moment to shine and they deserve it! It is the wise CEO who recognizes and encourages this!

CHAPTER EIGHT

*Places On The Planet -
Our Personal Space*

The Appetizer

Our personal surroundings play a significant role in our banquet. Each course, the appetizer, the main course and the dessert react quite differently to their environment. This extends to personal home space, work space and geographic places. We spend our entire lives dealing with these areas and their respective influences. Each of us, regardless of our course types, can use awareness to improve our ability to live with ourselves and others more harmoniously.

Let's begin, as always with the introductory appetizer. As we have previously discussed - the most significant quality all starters share is providing a stimulus for the main course which follows. Here's the interesting tidbit! These first course people need to develop an awareness of their output of energy. Many times there is a likelihood of "being all over the map." Too much! Since organization does not always seem present in their method of operation, great care should be directed toward simplifying their life. This begins with their surroundings. I shall explain. Using the symbology of the three course meal, the appetizer is quite simply, an invitation for the succulent offerings to follow. It is a mistake to overpower the diner in the beginning, yet this is a common tendency for this type. The art of moderation and pacing oneself needs to happen for the appetizer personality to be most effectual for themselves and others.

Beginning with the home, consider the space. The stimulating energy can easily be manifested in many objects overwhelming the physical space. The exact opposite is very helpful to this first course, minimizing possessions and keeping those possessions in their designated space.

Let's take a typical day in the life of the appetizer. Usually the day begins early, starters live up to their name. Most often they are not late or even long sleepers. Bright eyed and bushy tailed, they literally jump out of bed, ready for the day - which incidentally rarely goes as planned! One certainty with this type is that nothing is certain. Now, a word concerning diet. Coffee is usually not the best idea because a jolt of caffeine is the last thing this type needs. A soothing herbal tea, such as mint or chamomile is a far superior choice. Quiet réflective time is a great way to begin the day. Next, choosing a nourishing breakfast - not a quick smoothie or yogurt and fruit.

Now, there is nothing wrong with these choices for the other courses, but "a stick to the ribs " would be a wiser course in this case. The portion can be small but nourishing, grounding, and substantial.

Organizing the day's activities works well for this course. Why? Because the starter is very likely to have more activities in their head than can possibly be accomplished in an efficient, non - exhausting manner. One useful practice is to cross off all non - essential tasks, allowing if possible a little cushion of time for the absolutely necessary jobs. One may ask, "how can this be done when working in the office as opposed to being self - employed?" I agree it can be more challenging, however good management of one's business time translates in a higher quality of work and fewer mistakes. Bosses usually appreciate these traits in the long run.

Speaking of business - whether home or office, avoid having disarray in your work area. It is very disorienting to all types, but most of all to this one. Immediate use materials should be the only ones at your fingertips and within eyeshot. Handle these and then proceed to the next in order of importance. The difference in peace of mind is surprising.

Proceeding through the day, we come to the lunch break. Ah! Here is the challenge - Stop! It is vital to create an interruption in your workday to enjoy a proper meal. Again, it can be small, BUT not at your desk, or kitchen counter and definitely not snack food! If possible, take a quick walk to a park or an outside area - weather permitting. If this is not possible, find a place where you can relax. Your food should be appealing and nourishing. Do not make phone calls while eating, make it a time to recharge. In many countries of Europe, a two hour respite is built into the workday to accommodate a lovely lunch followed by a siesta! It works for them, think about that.

When the workday is completed, here we will pause to address the self-employed person, as many more are opting for this choice. One key to being successful entrepreneurs is to STOP working at a prescribed hour. Believe it or not, those who work for themselves often devote even longer hours with less break time. Make a schedule of time devoted to business and stick to it, except for dire emergencies and make sure they are rare. Evenings are important to relax and enjoy the evening meal, not just fast food take outs. If a social event is planned, some quiet downtime, if only a half an hour will refresh and prepare you to enjoy the event ahead of you. You will be much happier and others will benefit from your company.

Lastly, get a good night's sleep. That's a true fountain of youth for all of us, but even more so for the appetizer. They go at full speed most of the time, their battery really needs a recharge!

The Main Course

This is the substantial part of the meal, the course the appetizer prepares for and the dessert finalizes. The best - right? No, simply the main aspect of the three, at times a challenge as well. Main courses are usually the focal point of the dining experience. In life, they often attempt to claim center stage, literally! Quite frankly, this can be too much of a good thing. In life's associations this tendency must be tempered in the interests of harmony. At the moment, we are observing how this balance can be achieved in our personal space.

First, we will look at our home, the areas in which we live. This type would benefit from gentle choices. What does this mean? Initially, the color scheme should be soft rather than bold, not necessarily boring and neutral, but avoiding strong presentations of hues and patterns. Order within the space is also important for this course. More objects can be tolerated comfortably than for the appetizer, but having designated spaces, avoiding the tendency to hoard.

Main courses tend to be somewhat scheduled, however it is necessary to avoid rigidity and compulsion. It is also well to keep in mind that the other two types do not schedule or organize in the same fashion.

Now, we will observe the work space, whether in or out of the home. Main courses can very easily be work alcoholics! This, of course is not in their best interests. Why is this trait so common with this type? First, because of the tendency to be well organized and efficient. It is important that this central course remember they are not the only or best on the planet! A surprise tactic is to utilize, whenever possible the other two parts of the meal - namely the appetizer and dessert.

If this is a difficulty due to the fact one operates alone (self - employed) rather than as a business team, the act of creating diversions helps with inspiration and reaching a conclusion. A hobby or sport can fill the needs on either end. It is also vital to cut oneself some slack when creating schedules. Catch your breath time, if you will.

Let's talk about eating habits. Main courses are generally fast eaters, seldom taking time to savor the food or beverage. The usual result of this practice is to overeat or become a compulsive snacker. Sometimes, this type will skip a meal entirely to get more done. Why is this important? The answer is that these habits seriously diminish our productivity and in time one's very health itself.

Take time for a proper meal, three of them in fact! Regarding the specific types of food for each meal, the content can be light. Some examples can be fruit and yogurt for breakfast, or an egg and toast if desired. Lunch can be a salad with some protein. Dinner may comprise of a small carb plus a vegetable and a protein of choice. Some people prefer to eat their principal meal at midday. This is actually a great practice, however, it can be a bit more challenging with certain lifestyles. None of these meals need be large, the important thing is that a designated time and space is allotted. You will find the benefits very rewarding almost immediately!

Sleep may elude this principle or main course, as it does for the appetizer at times. It is vital to prepare oneself to relax in the evening. As we talked about with the appetizer, stop work at a prescribed time. Devote the evening to self - nurturing, whether alone or with others. If you go out with your significant other, or even close friends, be sure you are in an atmosphere you enjoy and find nurturing. Yes, sometimes we must consider others but, I believe not at the cost of one's own misery. Ask yourself if the association is worth your time. Weigh the pluses and minuses. Be honest with yourself and others, if possible in a kind and gentle manner. For example, if those close to us have very different tastes in food - is it possible to find a restaurant where options are offered that accommodate both of you? The same is true of entertainment and atmosphere. Some commonality must have brought you together. Explore these whenever possible. It can happen that we grow and change in a different way than those around us, therefore we must make decisions accordingly. You may be wondering why I am spending more time with these personality traits in this discussion of the second or main course. The reason is - this course is, in many cases, stronger impacting in a way the appetizer and dessert are not.

Ahhh - The Dessert

You may wonder why I usually preface the introduction of the dessert with ahhhh. It's because we do well with drawing a breath before this course. Finally we embrace the dessert in all its drama! The biggest challenge is the follow up to first, the tantalizing appetizer, and even more closely the strength of the main course. The purpose of the dessert is a sweet, lingering finale! How does this work in our daily world? This type of person often acts the part of the savior. They are designed to culminate the meal, but alas in our society this is often easier said than done.

The home surroundings of the dessert is often cozy and attractive however, in a scattered manner due to the fact there is a tendency towards overwhelm. They are so mindful of others that the fact they are not the saving grace (full meal) in and of themselves, there can be an energetic deficiency. The dessert was meant to literally wrap it up!

Let's apply this theory to the workplace, or the world of business. Generally, the finale functions best as part of a group as opposed to a "lone ranger" role. They are most useful as closers of all kinds, however, their forte does not include initiating the deal. Seldom do they excel at sales, however as attorneys they shine. Why? Consider this - lawyers have staff to do the groundwork and prepare the case. These are the starters and main courses. The final actions are taken by the attorneys to bring about a verdict. Closure - right? Another career is medicine, particularly surgeons. The patient is prepared by others for the final "Fix." You have realized, by this time, the dessert functions as the closing act of the play. They can shine in big productions or small ones. The important thing to remember is their role in accordance with the two vital roles preceding them.

In the daily life of a dessert, scheduling is one of the challenges. In the professions cited above this aspect is handled by the staff, however in personal matters chaos may occur. Meals need to be given proper time - not just coffee and quick snacks. It is essential to allocate time specifically dedicated to family and friends. Quiet alone time is also vital. Desserts tend, actually, to be quite social, but finding adequate space in their life is the problem. They can also be workaholics due to their savior complex.

The other side of the coin occurs when the final course lacks motivation. This usually occurs through physical or mental burn-out resulting in a form of depression. The dessert needs proper acknowledgement, both personally and in the work arena. It is relatively easy to fail to give proper credit to the final course. When this happens it is vital for the dessert to realize their own value and continue their important function.

The Global Scene - The Appetizer

Let's view these concepts on a global level. Distinctive areas clearly present themselves. Our journey begins in the United States, opening with the appetizer. The dramatic mountains ranging from east to west definitely fit this category! On the east coast to the north we have the Appalachians, then the Blue Ridge, highlighting the south. These are the gentle, time honored beginnings of our meal, tantalizing and awakening our senses. Moving west to the Rockies! Nothing subtle about those babies! Wow! A spiced, hot appetizer that occupies our attention and thrills our taste buds!

We then progress to the extreme west near the coast and embrace the Sierra Nevadas - more like a vichyssoise (potato - leek soup), intense and soothing simultaneously. Quite a combo! Which of these vistas appeal to each of us? Which speaks loudest to our palate? Let's look again at our choices. To begin our meal, do we want to be slowly seduced by our taste buds? Do we want to rock them? Do we want a little of both? The choice is ours to make. The answers are obvious. The gentle, more mellow mountains are the slow seductive choices. The western mountains, the rock-em choice. The coastal mountains of California, Oregon and Washington are the option for a mixture of drama and gentle - neither extreme.

The countries of Europe offer comparable terrain, from the Alps to the sloping mountains and hills. The rugged ancient terrain stretching across France and Italy, into Spain bringing fire to the blood of even the most timid of souls, satisfying those with an insatiable taste for the extreme!

Exploring Main Courses On The Planet

When we ponder the main course, the substantial part of our meal, what comes to mind? A quality of nourishment bringing a feeling of sustained fullness and comfort, making us feel satisfied, even a little ecstatic! This is precisely what our taste buds were primed for with the appetizer.

The terrain of the earth contains the same degree of nurturing. Where? Let's begin in America, then venture abroad. The farmlands of the Midwest, with it's wheat fields, corn and grassy plains dotted with sheep or cattle are one example. The very air of these areas, consciously cultivated, carry the balm of healing and wholeness similar to the coveted protection of a healthy childhood. Lakes often appear sporadically throughout these vistas. Greenery, so much greenery, in the form of fruit trees spread their boughs over the verdant grasses. Gardens heavy with berries and vegetables grace the countryside or snuggle the country houses. Farm stands pop up during the growing season, expressing the close bond of the inhabitants and the earth they work. Driving through envelopes one in a sense of serenity and strength. The purpose of the principal part of the meal.

As we journey abroad, we may choose to embrace the rolling agricultural areas of Europe. What can compete with the intoxicating ecstasy of the lavender fields stretching across Provence, France? The very air is indescribable in its heady fragrance! Vineyards transverse the lands surrounding the ancestral chateaux and the smaller manses. The senses are expanded even further by the orchards of olive trees weighed down with their luxurious harvest. The very backbone of life is held within these lands. Italy, Greece and Spain offer similar landscapes, presenting themselves for our pleasure!

The Finale -The Dessert

What qualities of a dessert speak to our senses? Perhaps the soothing, lingering, seductive sensations we want to savor, hold within our grasp! Despite our efforts, the pleasure is a fleeting experience, yet so worth the moment!

What aspects of the earth mirror these sensations the closest? Bring to mind a beach, its gentle lapping waves, succulent sand and azure skies with seagulls soaring overhead. What parallels exist in this slice of nature! Each such moment must be savored in and of itself, for its very attraction lies in an endless changing vista. Peace and tranquility one moment - then a tempest in the blink of an eye! How can this be compared to a dessert with its vast variety of moods? A dessert can also take many forms, from the soft gentle texture of creams to the drama of a flaming dish, plus a myriad of variations in between. The qualities they share however, easily identify with the final course.

The alluring sweetness that echo in our taste buds even when the flame burns off, releases the essence of the final finish. So, also the lull after the waves finish crashing the shore and the sun breaks through the dark clouds. We want to capture and hang onto the beauty of the beach areas, but one of two paths present themselves to us. One, our time in these resort areas is usually numbered. Our beachside holiday comes to an end, leaving us craving for more, as we often do with a luscious dessert, but knowing we must be satisfied for the present. Similarly we must acknowledge our delicious meal has reached its completion. Our second path is perhaps even a bit more frustrating. If we choose to create a life living day to day in this paradise, it becomes too rich in its pleasures for us to appreciate long term. We must take respites from its almost hypnotic effect.

Remember, the dessert is preceded by the appetizer and then the main course. For the sake of comparison, we must keep in mind the dessert is not a meal in itself!
It lacks the stimulus and the substance of the two preceding courses, therefore, it needs the qualities of stimulation and strength to complete the picture.

There are other aspects of nature that can give us the qualities of the dessert, especially if we are not beach or ocean people. One is a lush garden existing for the sole purpose of imparting beauty - food for the soul! Ideally, a garden contains a carpet

of grass, bushes laden with flowers, their myriad of
scents mingling in the air. Picture a bench waiting
to comfort you, filling you with a feeling of delicious serenity. A type of dessert is it not? The mar-
riage of colors and textures are truly a delight to the
being! This type of enfoldment is a very special type
of completion, the kind that is savored at the end
of a busy day transcending us into the late hours.
This is much like the final course of the meal lulls
us into the twilight time. Unlike the beach, the garden carries a more gentle energy, more continuity.
Lethargy may set in if great periods of time were
spent in its embrace. It is best savored in smaller
increments. Perhaps the best aspect of the garden
lies in one's ability to easily create such a haven. A
few artfully spaced pots of flowers, herbs or both
can be placed on a small city balcony or patio with
a bench, perhaps a table and chairs for those res-
torative moments. Taking time to have our meals in
such an atmosphere can be a valuable technique to
recharge our being. "Stopping to smell the flowers "
is a very truthful statement!

The desert, like the word dessert, for the finale
to our meal, have a great deal in common. Picture
a vast expanse of land, unobstructed by buildings,
as far as the eye can see. How like the sea it really
is, quite serene in its openness and absence of life!
In some cases, grasses or cacti are visible but, even
they have an aspect of nakedness. It is said that the
best exercise for the eyes is to expose them to such
stretches of landscape, counteracting the stress of

close - up visual demands. I believe it goes beyond this theory, allowing relaxation for the entire organism.

Another gift of nature - truly revitalizing in a peaceful way is a forest, with its sweeping arms of green and scent of pine permeating the senses! The calming energy of a walk through a forest is unparalleled in its serenity. An almost primitive energy replacing the frenetic energy we often find ourselves in the midst of. At times, the additional gift of wild berries or healing present themselves, if we are skilled in recognizing these marvels of nature!

We have talked about the ocean, but there is another gift of water - an inland lake, refreshing and comforting at the same time. The lake bottom, whether it's pebbles or sand. Sometimes abounding with fish and boats, yet retaining a feeling of sweetness and intimacy. The provincial surroundings of lakes draw a somewhat different energy than the sea, less intimidating - more accessible. Sometimes appearing after descending the crest of a small hill. There it is, nestled at its base awaiting and inviting! Lakes appear in a variety of terrains, mountains, plains, forests and even farmlands. The trait they have in common is tranquility. Yes, it is true they can be restless at times, but it is short - lived, soon returning to its stillness. Sitting by a lake is a romantic experience whether alone or in the company of another, just as a luscious dessert can be enjoyed in solitude or with company. Some people even go so far as to say they can savor certain ex-

periences more deeply in solitude! Freeing thought
- isn't it?

Now we will explore the different climates that
surround these environments. They certainly echo
the three courses we are discussing.

Hot weather sets the stage for more intensity,
much like the appetizer. Before the advent of air
conditioning, the daily way of life reflected the
need for keeping the body as comfortable as possible by moderating the body's temperature. This
is reflected in the architecture, building with cross
ventilation. The use of trees, wherever possible,
promoted shade, giving relief from the sun's rays.
The main activities of the day took place in the
early morning or evening. The siesta, actually a
great practice, took place in the middle of the day
in certain countries. This respite during the day,
which never caught on in the U.S., was based on a
survival ethic that leaves out downtime. Interesting how the countries that respect the quality of
balance in life are still perking along.

Clothing reflects the climates as well. This
is demonstrated by the traditional white flowing
dress of the desert peoples and even the pastels in
other places. The climate control we experience
actually brings into play another course which we
will take up in more detail at a later point.

Temperate climates, which comprise the majority of the earth's terrain, parallel the qualities of the
main course. Feelings of groundedness and nourishment carry us onwards without either stimulus

or lethargy. It's true, the temperate parts of the earth's geography do not always remain moderate, however the climbing temps and dipping lows are usually short-lived. The likeness of the main course is similar. We feel nourished and satisfied. These temperate zones also usually reflect a feeling of security, very helpful to our sense of well-being.

Lastly, we embrace the dessert. The succulent cocoon of warm trade winds and tropical moisture herald the dessert! These areas are the escape from the more intense weather. Even the warmth is not usually excessively hot, which is why I placed them in the dessert category. Generally these climes are near water, but the distance may extend inland a bit. Interesting, as in the experience of the final course for our meal, most people do not choose to surround themselves with this experience on a constant basis. The wisdom of shorter getaway times is best. Remember our meal comparison - too much dessert is just that - too much of a good thing. We enjoy small doses much more. People who have located more permanently in this setting would do well to take their getaway to climates exhibiting the appetizer or main course, thus creating a balance of their own somewhat in reverse. Since experiencing their dessert first, it is appropriate to round out their "meal" with the experience of the appetizer or main course.

The elements of nature merit a reflection as well. They follow both the places and the climates, but slightly transcend them, as well as adding drama to our meal.

Rain is an interesting example, which actually can be a meal in itself! A thunder and lightning storm is - you guessed it, a zesty appetizer! A steady downpour, with its nourishment for the earth, is - yes the main course. Lastly, but not least, the sweet gentle rain followed by a rainbow is our dessert! We will show, in the second part of the book, how we can truly enjoy this lovely gift of nature in its full potential.

Close following the rain is it's frozen twin the snow! The snow can be three courses, as well. The wild blizzard laying down drifts of snow, usually accompanied with wind, is certainly the spicy appetizer, filled with ramifications if we have too much! The gentle falling snow, quietly depositing a blanket of whiteness upon the ground transforming the landscape into a fairyland, is surely a main course! We want to just snuggle into our abode, read and indulge in nourishing foods, feeling secure and tranquil. How is this white stuff a dessert? The end result of this winter wonderland is best enjoyed by a walk, embracing the beauty, or by getting our hands in by building a snowman for the young at heart! How about skiing or snowboarding? Lovely in its gifts is this picturesque element we call snow!

Wind, this versatile element can also cover the entire meal. Brush winds preceding weather changes fit perfectly into the appetizer course. This aspect of wind never lasts too long. It is too dramatic and sometimes damaging as in the case of tropical storms or tornadoes. Similarly, a highly spiced starter can give one indigestion if we overly indulge. On the other hand, a steady, gentle breeze is a balm to our senses. It can rustle the leaves or ripple the waves enhancing our sensory pleasures, as does the main course. The balm of the wind stays with us even after the direct experience has passed. The taste of our final course affects us in like fashion.

Fire is a wild, wonderful gift of nature. When governed and controlled, it is so useful, even needed. Unleashed it is a fury to behold! The wildfire is a very strong kin to the appetizer - harsh and strong, but making a clear path for new growth in its wake! I realize this is an extreme example, but there is a resemblance. Now, picture the fire in a fireplace or stove, warming the house or even able to cook our food. Our ancestors worshipped fire because for them, it represented the sustainment of life itself! When fire was first discovered, there are many different theories regarding its origins - it literally changed the course of mankind! It made foods more easily consumed and climates previously difficult for habitation possible, even in the cold months of the year. How like the main course brings nourishment and comfort to the body. The very gentle use of fire can be witnessed in the use of candle flame, again a cultural phenomenon. This firelight, beginning with torches then progressing to candlelight literally illuminated dark places and the night itself. Even today, we cherish the sweetness of candlelight, inspiring romantic feelings and lingering pleasure - ahhh - the dessert!

Our final element to ponder is earth itself! We will explore its versatility and gifts to our meal. The ground we tread is endlessly varied, with the extreme qualities of its plant, animal and mineral kingdom. Beneath it are housed wonders in the form of subterranean rivers and caves, with stalactites and stalagmites, sometimes dating back to prehistoric times. How does all this fit into our scheme of things regarding our three course meal? Actually quite dramatically! The nature of the earth is very adaptable - basically accommodating to its creatures whenever possible. Let's narrow our scope to some specifics.

The frozen ground of the northern climates bring a jolt to the senses much like an appetizer, preparing the life producing time of spring. The soil then awakens and progresses into the height of its full maturation time of summer. This is truly a time of comfort and well being reminiscent of our main course. The earth is virtually pulsating with life and substance! The time of harvest is heralded by the fall of the year. The final crops are harvested. The ground has spent itself for the nourishment of its creatures! The sweet finale of autumn is the dessert before the rest and repose of winter. When we linger with our final course, reminiscing over our meal before we end our day, so does the earth before the winter.

PART TWO

CHAPTER NINE

Evolution of an Appetizer

Now that we have an overall picture of our meal, we shall look deeply into the journey of life within each of our three courses.

The appetizer, always the beginning - The Baby! Yes, an appetizer is apparent from the moment of movement in the womb! No way - you say! See if this rings a bell, you moms out there. Let's cruise through the array of starters on those menus. Many different types greet our eye. In the U.S. salads of varied combinations are usually offered. In the European countries, there exists a slightly different order. Salads are usually offered to clear the palate before the final cheese and dessert, but we will include them in our array of starters due to the fact that is how they are widely featured in America. Perhaps the thought may be to prepare the palate and stimulate it simultaneously. My observation is also that generally a more distinctive dressing is used in this case. The salad type of person is generally lighter energetically, but nonetheless carrying a particular titillating invitation to the main course. The assortment of spicy choices in this category hold no mystery regarding the path toward the next balancing course. Seafood may also be offered in the beginning- a more gentle seductive opener paving the road to the full bodied main course.

We shall begin to draw the parallel regarding our new person making its entrance into the world. The infant exhibiting appetizer qualities can run the gamut of the traits mentioned above. The moments in utero are usually decisive, unpredictable and a bit restless. This wonderful little being shows an eagerness to get on with it! With what, you may ask? The business of life - first and foremost- getting born! It's really a big deal, especially for this beginner type. If the mother is also an appetizer, it can be a bit challenging, but she can certainly rise to the occasion! The optimal course of action would be to expose herself to the emotional aspects of the main course whenever possible. This can be accomplished by human personalities, or even environmental energies. It isn't unusual for main course types to couple with starters for the mutual benefits of the balance of energies.

During the pregnancy, the main course energy offers a much needed stabilizing emotional climate. If the father happens to be this grounding source - wonderful! A word of wisdom here though, the main course needs to stay strong to enable him to give his support. How can this be accomplished?

First, and foremost, by recognizing his need to do so. Sports activities in short, small doses are invaluable, particularly those which offer solitude or quite camaraderie with dessert types. Why? Dessert types are soothing and calming, unlike the stimulating effect of the appetizer partner.

Now, please know all of these energies are wonderful in and of themselves however, the magic component is balance. Brief moments spent in the ways mentioned enable the main course to return to the company of the starter with a renewed vigor to share.

Let's consider the case if the partner is an appetizer as well. This is indeed a tricky trio, the mom, the infant in utero, and dad - a truly powerful scenario, rare but possible. Awareness is key in this situation, since both partners must be tuned in to prevent energy burnout. This is rather easily recognized if fatigue or irritability rears its head. The important action is to be sensitive and intercept these conditions before they become full bloom. Pay close to eating nutritionally at regular intervals. These types can become so involved in activities that they literally forget to eat - very unwise. Relaxed meals in pleasant surroundings are important. Equally vital are periods of rest. It is a wonderful practice to take a little time in the afternoon to "kick back." Ideally this should be done relaxing in the bedroom, phone and computer off! Perhaps a little light reading is ok, feel free to close your eyes and drift off if possible. The comment is often made "oh, I can't nap during the day, I won't sleep well at night." Can entire European countries who consider two hour lunches and siestas be wrong? Perhaps a more jovial outlook on life is helped by this custom. In any event - try it! Another revitalizing practice is a walk in nature, or even sitting in the garden or on the patio. As you might have detected each of these actions have elements in common, quietness and peace. I also suggest they be done alone.

The infant in utero also receives the restful vibes which will evidence themselves as more relaxed, easier babies.

The next parent combo is the dessert, when a dessert dad couples with a starter baby and a starter mom, interesting right? This is how it may play out. This final course - the dessert adds a nice finishing touch, literally and figuratively. But, desserts are meant to follow the main course. In this scenario, with the mom as the starter, the infant as the starter and dad the dessert, where is the main course? Again, this is a less often happening in energetic coupling, but it does happen! Most important is the need for an addition of strength and grounding in the mix. This is not an obvious awareness in this trio. How is this achieved? Let's look to our surroundings and activities. Our home needs to nurture us, how can this be played out? The use of soothing colors in our decor, not too vibrant or too bland, with soothing furniture kept neat and uncluttered. The outside space should also radiate a rejuvenating energy, rather than stimulating or boring. The size dimensions of our living quarters are less important than how we handle it. If we live in a city, it is vitally important that we pay attention to carve out our niche that gives us these qualities. In the countryside, the very essence echoes these attributes.

We will now move onto infancy and childhood with the appetizer, showing different ways to navigate these developmental phases.

Childbirth may be a bit dramatic with the appetizer baby. He or she is quite eager to get on with it, but at the same time needs to adapt to the situation at hand, namely the mom giving birth! The starter is a bit of a solo act and having his / her debut occurring in the throes of a mutual effort is a bit of a trip for this particular energy. Patience and endurance are the keys here, I must venture to stress! All in good time and usually with a bit of pomp this little one will make a presence. A lusty howl is a great beginning, then a suckle should launch this little one. In the case of any necessary medical intervention, it is well to bear in mind this energy is a strong one and usually all will be well.

The appetizer needs to remember that he/she is not a solo act, but a group player, if only with the parents. Attention to the infant is vital, but equally so, integration into the scheme of life. What do I mean by this? I am a firm believer in the marsupial handling of infants. What does this imply? Nurse on demand and wear the infant in a wrap or carrier tending to life as usual. This may sound confining, but trust me - I have raised four children this way and it is freeing! Unlike foals and baby whales, we humans are not able to be solo till we can crawl at least - somewhere after six months. Ancient people used this method and it served them well! Many ask - where does the father fit in this scheme of things? Well, he can wear the baby as well! There are many excellent books on this subject. My point is that the baby is integrated into the family's activities and can sleep on the go, rather than becoming a tyrant and dictating the schedule of his parents. The starter child can do this more assertively than the other courses, actually. The other plus of this method is the stimulation experienced effortlessly by being the bystander in adult activities - just by being carried along! The additional benefit is that the parents do not feel robbed of their life by having a baby.

Let's look at this wonderful being moving into childhood. Now, that's a trip! Appetizers take "the bull by the horns!" This translates into not only embracing life's adventures but actually taking charge and creating them. The different ways this is experienced by the parents may look like this. Physical development, such as crawling and walking usually takes the speed of a wildfire once the basic skills are mastered. " A mile a minute" can be the case, wow! How do we as parents deal with this? The answer varies with the course type of the parent. If the parent is a starter, he/she can be perfectly comfortable with the energetics, however, the important thing is that the scenario not be increased. Okay, what does this mean? Simply, that the parent with similar characteristics recognize this and balance themselves with energies of the other courses of the meal, namely the main course (substantial and grounding) and the dessert (soothing and sweet). As we have previously shared, this can be accomplished in different ways. If the person or persons around us exhibit these qualities-great! If this is not the case, we need to utilize other influences to do so, as described earlier.

Main course parents will have a different perspective regarding their exciting child. These can range from proud observation to exhausting frustration. Actually, a main course parent can be very helpful to a little appetizer. Remember, they comprise the first two courses of the meal. The concern here is that the main course does not burn out in the process. Remember, this substantial course can sometimes stretch themselves too thin! In which case, this too must be addressed and steps taken to lighten up and self-care. Dessert activities or people accomplish this nicely.

Speaking of desserts, what if the parent is the dessert type? This makes for an interesting scenario. The typical role of the dessert is to bring a soothing sweetness to the meal. This translates, in this case, to a quiet peaceful time after the activity of the little one. Cuddles and gentle moments can bring a sweet finish to the toddler's busy day preparing for sleep. These times are extremely vital to the emotional growth and balance of all children and particularly for the appetizer child. What happens to the person acting in this role as the parent? The necessary balance element for the dessert is the healing and strength of the main course. This can be done by life style and/or associations. We talked, before of the role diet and eating patterns play in this nurturing. To review briefly, the dessert needs people, places and environments of sustenance to carry out their role as the sweet finish.

Next, we will continue our banquet to embrace the older childhood years with our appetizer. Ah! The beginning of independence! The terrible twos can be traced to this feeling. The child has proven to himself or herself that they are a separate being and can have autonomy. It is, however, much more limited than the child realizes. Now, in the case of the appetizer, the zest for life continues. The role of the parent is to encourage - yet limit this independence. Here is where the classic role of child rearing and new philosophies butt heads. Perhaps, the old fashioned way was too heavy handed, literally and physically. The current trend, however, can be definitely found to lack structure and necessary boundaries. There is a reason that, unlike members of the animal kingdom, humans have an infinitely longer developmental process. Even when a child is capable of simple tasks and by all means should be encouraged to engage in them for himself/ herself and others, does not mean they should run the show. The starter personality may attempt this more readily than the other two courses. This is by no means a negative move, but boundaries must be set for everyone's sanity and well-being. What does this entail? A family structure is vital to any society! In our dynamics of sometimes a single parent and working families, does this seem impossible? Many people simply don't bother, giving up in frustration. It can be done! What is necessary is creative thought. Does it take effort? Yes, anything worthwhile does! It is said that all efforts spent in rearing well-adjusted children will free the parents from a lifetime of dependent, dysfunctional children in adult bodies to deal with in their golden years.

I believe the flow of this theory does not have to be rigid in the least, but the child needs to know that someone is calling the shots. Even though it may look like he/she wants to, it is vital that they know the parent is the one who is truly in charge.

Mealtimes, culturally have been gathering times and I believe, this to be an important aspect of daily life that the child can depend on. The meal time should be a time of sitting down together, taking precious moments to share at whatever level is appropriate. This should be done AWAY from electronic devices at all costs! I am not a believer in strict bedtime schedules. I feel it is too limiting to possible family activities. That being said, if the child needs to get up at a specific hour, then of course proper hours of sleep must be had.

School days are made to order for the appetizer. A ready and eager learner with a burning desire to participate are some sterling qualities that make this experience a delight. The key guidelines are again, keeping oneself nourished and sustained in more ways than one, keeping an eye for this youth to also be balanced in their lifestyle. Music, dance, sports and family activities are all opportunities to channel the exuberance of the appetizer pre-teen. Emotional ups and downs are par for the course during this period of growth. A listening ear and strong guidelines are the keynotes to avoiding pitfalls. Unfortunately, in this modern age, the pre-adolescent years embrace more challenges than in previous eras. My personal feeling is a strict monitoring of hi-tech devices is crucial to appropriate social development. I will not dwell on this subject, but I will say the best way to address this challenge is by parental example. These examples include NOT multitasking by half listening to your child while still having your phone in hand! Give them your undivided attention! Discipline yourself to specific times on your computer. Taking time to live life fully. "Actions speak louder than words" is an old but good adage!

A very popular concept in new thought parenting is what I call "the cheerleader." Positive support for the accomplishments of your young person is very important, but over the top exuberance for every little thing that is done, diminishes the impact of the more outstanding victories they accomplish. Young people are very quick to spot insincerity and lack of validity if compliments are overdone. Often, the parent compensates their lack of consistent involvement with their children by this repetitive cheering. It is perfectly appropriate to offer, when necessary, very gentle constructive criticism. First, and foremost, one of the prime roles of a parent is loving guidance. Appetizers benefit greatly from this action because of their zestful approach to the "meal of life."

Let's travel on to those delightful teen years with our appetizer. Now, the party begins! Be prepared to attend all the sporting events. Your appetizer will probably be a member of the team, or quite possibly-the captain! Actually, this is a very positive outlet for the bursts of energy this course possesses. It's a bit like a wind up toy from the old days (before battery operated). They are either full of energy or asleep. It's a wise decision to find a strategy to enjoy or at least survive this way of being. Embracing the cheering section can be great fun with the victories, however, consoling the losses can present a challenge. The starters do not do well with what appears as defeat, usually feeling a bit of depression. The good news is that it never lasts long until they are literally charged again.

What is the state of passage for the modern teen? The car - the driver's license fills this moment! Ahhh! A new stress for the parent! Fortunately the driver training has been given over to the professionals. That's a good thing, I believe, not because a parent is not qualified to teach, but let's face it -who needs the stress. Be grateful this task can be done by others and your nerves and car escape the risk! Now the course is aced and license in hand, what's next? Boundaries! First and foremost, the exuberance of the appetizer on the open road can manifest as speed and risk taking! I firmly believe a way to circumvent this drama is for the teen to get a job. Even in this day and age, there is work that can be had. The pay is not so much the issue, as using that wonderful energy especially present in the appetizer. Secondly, gifting the teen with a car is a very unwise choice. Cars should be earned and car expenses, such as gas and insurance should be the responsibility of the driver! Before your youth has his own car, the driving should be dealt out with discretion. The gas should be paid by the driver, when he /she uses it as preparation for car ownership in the future.

All said and done, most survive this period unscathed! Academics should be monitored and most importantly social interactions. Teens are trying their wings, but hopefully they have not flown the nest yet and there is a good reason. The physical bodies are ready, creating challenges, but the relationship between cause and effect needs more tweaking.

Eighteen comes soon, and in our culture marks a rite of passage. This is the time when the woman or man is recognized as mature and capable of making their own decisions regarding their lives. This is somewhat compromised today, due to the fact many young adults are still being supported by their parents while attending college. This is actually a delayed adolescence. I firmly believe the costs of college, to whatever degree possible, should be handled by the students themselves. Oh! I hear the arguments already! How can my daughter or son have the energy to maintain good grades and work? That's the point! If they are taught independence must be earned by contributing to the costs of their education, they will have less time and energy for mischief! This is especially true for the starter course.

We will now applaud their true adulthood. Our focus shifts to the key player- the appetizer, their young adult years and possible choices.

Some young adults actually skip the college scene or do not seek to complete it in the years directly following their high school years. Alternative schooling is having a strong impact on education and in most cases, a very beneficial one. If either of these choices are the ones of your starter, I applaud them! Approaching the school of life, practically or formally, such as re-entering college as an adult, apprenticeship, or forging a path of their own demonstrates an ability to embrace life to its fullest! This is true as long as the practical and financial responsibilities are undertaken by the emerging adult.

The appetizer may have an interesting experience with affairs of the heart. With his/her dive in approach to life, some rocky coves are inevitable. The ability to make it to safe ground is a saving grace for the starter types. True love may seem rather elusive since most appetizers are true romantics. The chief detour lies in their tendency to be easily distracted. Usually the discovery is made that all that glitters is indeed not gold! Once truly in love, the starter is likely to give her/his all and hang in there.

Careers are another journey with a special twist for this type. Motivation is a key quality which goes a long way to insure their success. Often, the starter is an entrepreneur. Why? The answer lies in the fact that they are indeed the opening act. They are great in launching a project and their enthusiasm is literally contagious to their customers or clients. One of the ways the appetizer shines in the corporate world is sales or promotions. A problem with this situation occurs when too many controls are placed on them. This causes frustration and stifles both their creativity and innovative spirit. Many times the success this type brings to a company inspires promotion to management positions. This is usually a poor choice for the same restrictive reasons, and in addition, encourages "burn out." The appetizer does well with his own enterprise as long as the hands on aspect remains literally in their hands, with delegation of the supporting tasks. Many of the world's wealthiest people fit this slot.

Now, that our appetizer has succeeded in their respective career, what's next?

In today's world, many times careers occur during the middle years, hence, mid - life crisis. This is particularly true of the starters. How to avoid changes becoming crises - that is the question. The key here, is to sustain one's energy. This can be done by both discipline and balance. These two words may be thought of as an anthem to the appetizer, but in truth are vital to their health and longevity! Over scheduling and lack of maintaining consistency in their self-care are the weak areas of the starters. The remedy is pure Fun! This can take many forms, but the main aspect must be that it is relaxed and not achievement based. Since appetizers love a challenge, they often mistakenly think a workout in a gym, a strenuous hike or competitive sport recharges them. Wrong! These activities have their place, as we will discover, but not in this case. What really works is a stroll thru the park-literally, a slowly eaten meal in lovely surroundings, even reading a dreamy novel. Oh! I can hear the moans from you appetizers out there who down an expensive meal in minutes and probably can't remember when you did not bike or run to cover ground. I challenge you to try these suggestions and feel the revitalization that occurs. Cars were not meant to run in high gear all the time the motor is turned on. What occurs is that the engine burns out even with high test gas. That describes what is going on with our bodies when we run them in this fashion.

Let's shift out attention to travel to reset the energy meter. What fills the best slot for the starter people out there? Beaches! Yes beaches are the first choice for the appetizer type. Why? Water has a soothing effect for all of us, but for these dear ones, it's a balm for the soul! I am not talking high - powered water activities, but the tranquil communion with the lake or ocean, preferably less turbulent bodies of water. The tropical climate is also much more soothing than the jagged dramatic coastal areas. They have their place, as you will soon discover, when we discuss the other courses. Even if you are not a bather, walks along the sand will restore the spirit. Watching the panorama of the sunrise or sunset is a most rewarding experience. Well and good you may say, but I am a long distance from the sea, with no vacation funds at hand- what can I do? Good question! Most often there are inland lakes, man-made or natural, to gaze upon or weather appropriate, dip into even for an hour or whatever time you can manage. Pools or hot tubs are another option. If these are not available, how about a peaceful garden with water flowing if only a fountain. A last resort is to have a small fountain in your home to focus on, undisturbed, for a short time each day. Whether the grand vacation option, or the humble home fountain, the key is to expose yourself to this water energy whenever possible.

Ok, so you are a land lover- next option - provincial areas of rolling hills, pastures or small villages. You may detect some similarities among these geographic choices. Most definitely! The nature of a starter is always dramatic. A blessing and a curse. The invigorating energy for these starters is gentle, calming and beautiful! Rugged, majestic landscapes, however gorgeous, merely increase the tendencies of the appetizer, rather than complement them. Another aspect, to note, is the populated areas. Notice, I mentioned small villages or towns, not busy cities! The stimulation of metropolitan areas can be very attractive for this course, however, they should be avoided for that very reason. Appetizers create drama! It is their nature and their value in our "banquet of life," but to sustain the energy to contribute and to accomplish this, their batteries need to be re-charged by experiencing their polar opposites. Bon Voyage!

Next, we will embrace the appetizers as baby boomers! "The Golden Years" of today illustrates seventy is the new fifty! Nothing could be more truly said for the appetizer, if care has been taken to prevent burnout. We have shared how to nourish and replenish. Enthusiasm and zest for life , the trademarks of this course, can create a rich and rewarding experience during later life. There are a few points of caution. One, is to be gentle with oneself regarding physical activities, perhaps a little less strenuous and goal oriented, embracing a slightly more laid back attitude. This can seem like anathema for the starter person, striving to be the first in a race, climb the highest mountain or raft the wildest river. The competitive streak, so significant with the appetizer, can also rear its head in the world of business! Retirement can spell doom, gloom and boredom. Is there an alternative? Yes, either scale down own's career demands and keep a finger in, or find a new area of expertise that is enticing and productive. This keeps the juices flowing, both mentally and physically. Studies show new areas of learning benefit the brain and keep seniors alert! The main thing is to keep a positive outlook and be realistic at the same time.

Nutrition plays a key role in this drama as well. Food is an essential source of enjoyment, having said that, I feel moderation is the key to this aspect of life. Unless a specific food is deemed harmful due to a diagnosed condition, we can enjoy a variety, but as with all courses, quality and purity are most vital. Sometimes it is tempting for baby boomers to use prepared microwaved meals. Nooo! Portions need to be small. Older bodies process food more slowly, so the nutritional benefits must be closely adhered to. To sum it up, we all need to enjoy life to the fullest with responsibility to ourselves and others.

The last hurrah for the appetizers is likely to be in a blaze of drama, some more - some less. Just know this is simply in accord with the zest of a life lived their way! That's as good as it gets, right?

CHAPTER TEN

Evolution of the Main Course

Next on our menu is The Main Course! We have given the big picture regarding this course, but now we are going to hone in on the particulars.

Let's begin with the in utero experience. Remember the main course has strength and stability as it's cornerstone.This little embryo will most likely be quite a breeze during gestation, with strong rather predictable movements in the womb, and little drama in the pregnancy. If the mom is a starter, she may experience feelings of contentment and wellbeing. A need for more sleep may present itself, not because of a drain from the little beings existence as much as a genuine balance for her overactive lifestyle - a balance literally from within. A slightly different feeling is the case when the expectant mom is also a main course. Since both energies- that of the fetus and mom are so similar, there will be a flow. This is very positive, however, care must be taken if lethargy rears its head. Daily walks, rich in visual stimulation and beauty are wonderful. Work can and should continue, but with moderation. As the pregnancy advances, a siesta is highly beneficial, but not couch potato habits.

Ahhh-the dessert mom. Yes, I usually preface this food course with an ahhh! The pairing of these two courses in maternity is an easy one. Only a few obstacles can be noted. The dessert type is basically soft and smooth (crème brûlée), but does lack the solid aspect of the main course and the zest of the starter. These conditions can be easily remedied. In the case of the father being a main course, his input goes a long way to accomplish this. Pregnancy can seemingly create food cravings, and although all the courses experience this, it is more significant with the dessert mom. Care needs to be taken to eat main course type foods and temper the quick fix nutrient deficient ones. Exercise is vital for this course since they may be more sedentary, even more so than the main course. Undue exertion and some forms of movement are dangerous during pregnancy, so use discretion! Limiting screen time is important for all types, but especially for the dessert due to the fact they are prone to being spectators. Onward to the moment of birth for the main course. They set their own stage! Birth is a combined effort, mom, babe and hopefully dad too! Now, this course likes to get the mission accomplished without undue drama and hopefully no unnatural interference. Remember, I did not stress the duo or trio involved here. The reason is this type is not a team player by nature. They want to run the show with subordinates assisting them. Their entrance into the world is their first co-operative experience! Having said that, let's move on with this precious being.

Generally they are easy infants due to the fact they tend to be self regulated in their eating and sleeping habits, without undue fuss. Now, let's look at the family courses in detail. If the mom is a starter, the high point is she will tend to be a bit of a social dictator. She will take great delight in introducing her baby to new experiences and people. This is wonderfully stimulating to the main course, however, as with everything balance is the key. The main course desires order and rhythm in their life and too much stimulation can be irritating to them. Just as the appetizer thrives on stimulation, but needs the balance of calmness, the main course relates to an ebb and flow much like the ocean. Rigidity is not a flow, nor are surfing waves! This boy/girl will not hesitate to express their needs. Once those needs are met - such as eating, physical love and caring, they will nod off into sleep time. It is not necessary to adhere to a strict routine with these infants, in fact it is not advisable. There are specific reasons for this. Namely, these little ones are by nature self-regulated, therefore allowing the space for more flexibility, while maintaining order and stability. Chaos will result in problematic reactions from the infant. Above all, the appetizer mom needs to cut herself some slack, giving herself time to "let it all hang out" with creating personal time.

Let's look at the father's role in this meal. If the

father is a starter, as well as the mother (which is seldom the case) it would look a bit like a wildfire with the infant in the middle. By this illustration, I mean cooling energy needs to be brought into the picture. Calmness and steadiness must be manifested with the parents going to lengths to create their own method of easing their own energy. We will now look at the father as a fellow main course. This is actually a match that balances quite well. You can scarcely have too much stability and calmness, particularly when the mom is an appetizer. It will minimize her anxiety level as well as the infant's. She will be able to play her part more easily, yet provide the needed stimuli to the main course father and child. Another factor to keep in mind is that in most cases, the mother will be spending more hours with the infant, so there is little chance of lethargy exhibiting itself. The final possible scenario is the dessert father. As you now surmise, this constitutes the full three course banquet. What could be more perfect, right? It does make for a smooth flowing meal, but remember that the main course infant is strong and substantial, however underdeveloped in its flavors. This resembles a superb main course that has not simmered long enough for the full development of its flavors and textures. Translated this means that when bumps occur in this trio, it is simply because of the infantile status of the main course. What is the remedy for this situation? Unlike a meal - we cannot simply put it back on the stove, but we can allow time for development of potential flavors. This will happen naturally as time goes on, provided care is taken for proper development. The role of the parents, in this case as always, is in using awareness to complement their individual course types with the necessary energies to enhance their ability to enjoy the family meal, while picking up any slack their baby needs.

Moving into childhood and pre - school years, is our next step with this main course little one. Main course children naturally do well in school. Homeschooling is a great option also, because this course adapts to gentle structure. Since they are by personality predisposed to order and calmness (although order can be in the eyes of the beholder) they are less challenging to teach, or as I like to say introduce wisdom! They are not easily frustrated or distracted. This is the main challenge for all teachers, home or conventional school. Alternative schools, such as Waldorf or Montessori also work in this case. Unlike appetizer children, who do well with slightly more structure, the main course child seems to have an internal rhyme that keeps them on track. I shall deviant for a moment. There is no need to hesitate to try homeschooling or alternative schooling with an appetizer. If such is chosen, just keep in mind more scheduling can be helpful. Main course children are natural achievers, some may be overachievers. In this case, a quality diversion should be introduced- Not video games or movies! Interactive board games are superior to pushing keyboards! Board games necessitate interaction with others, sadly lacking in our children's lives as a whole!

Let's check in on the parent's role. Mom - first just kick back, no need to be a social director! When mom is an appetizer, this role can easily be her way. However well meaning, this course of action can be overwhelming for the main course. He/ she may even seek a bit of alone time in nature, in a completely safe atmosphere. Taking a deep breath for this type of mom works well, while reflecting at given moments. When the mom is a main course - it's a bit like "old home week." The similarity between mother and child makes the energy exchange a bit easier. It is wise, however, to remember as in infancy, we are still dealing with a course that is in the becoming stage - not fully developed yet. This calls for pulling rank at times. Parents should not strive to be friends, this is a great injustice to the young person. When there is the same course energy, this can be a tendency. In the case of mom being a dessert, we have a different dynamic. The child can attempt to overpower the meal, similar to the main course starter combo, but with a different twist. There is a time for a sweet finish to the meal, that is the purpose of the last course. Wrapping it up, calling a halt to activities and creating space for down time accomplishes this nicely. This can take the form of naps, quiet story time or bedtime. All of these are vital aspects to maintaining the strong sustaining energy of the main course child.

The father's role can follow the same guidelines, depending on his course type as well.

Now, charging ahead to adolescence. Main course children are in the final stages of development. The main course is almost fully prepared in all its strength and sustenance. The key word here is Almost! The flavors are tantalizing and the dish is so tempting. Parenting reaches a very challenging moment at this juncture. Why? Because the main course has been fairly predictable and stable throughout childhood, scholastically and socially. This type of teen is now ready to launch - not quite! Boundaries must be set in place for their own well being. The trend today in parenting is the buddy system. I have mentioned this earlier, but it bears repeating. The legal age of eighteen is set for a reason and that may be rushing things for some main courses. I stress this fact because the main course is a person of action and purpose! The final vestiges of maturation helps this impulse follow a positive direction. Main courses are the entrepreneurs of tomorrow as well as the CEOs, doctors and lawyers. The real challenge is that they do not become dictators in their way of handling their chosen fields. The course is on the table in all its glory and succulence. The parents can allow themselves to assume a less active role and now enjoy the advisory position.

The main course is prime for certain careers. They shine in positions where they have qualified starters and desserts to make their career responsibilities easier. I shall elaborate, for example, let's begin with the entrepreneur, owning one's own business. The ability to delegate is vital to this course and sometimes it is not natural for them. There is a tendency to be under the assumption they can do it all. Ego is both a blessing and a curse for this course. Even though they are the strongest part of the meal, their biggest threat is burnout. This occurs because they mistakenly assume there is no limit to their energy - wrong!

Even the proprietor of a small business will enhance his enterprise, plus his life by choosing assistants and listening to them. Before her/his business can support this payroll, there are ways to gain assistance from others. Apprenticeship is one, even volunteers can come forth if the vision is there. How many times have we witnessed a man or woman who has made their mark in the world and ended up sacrificing the very quality of their existence! Appetizers are made to bring business to the table, as in the banquet, thus preparing for the next course - the main course. The dessert is perfect for wrapping up the project sweetly. This leaves the main course to hold the center - the bigger picture, as the components round out the first and last course. This calls for some humility and definitely maturity for the main course, especially in private business. The corporate world, interestingly is pre-set this way. The CEO knows his/her role. In the case of skills in this arena, they acknowledge their starters and desserts, choosing them for compatibility as well as expertise. As with a lovely meal, where all the courses complement and enhance each other, such does a company which embraces these principles.

Sadly, this is not always the case. Chaos happens when a person assumes a role who is the wrong course for that position. Hopefully, this is remedied with a replacement role they are correctly fitted for. Professions follow this same dynamic, if we look closely. The lawyer, for example, has paralegals to be the starters, doing the groundwork by preparing the case with accompanying documents. Sometimes clients fail to understand this division of labor, complaining about not having the attorney do it all. It is important to realize that the most efficient method of accomplishing any task is to use talents most economically. The main course - the lawyer can then devote his knowledge and concentration where it is most needed. The final result can be recorded and carried out by the dessert very succinctly.

The next profession brilliantly illustrating these principles is that of the medical doctor. The nurses and technicians, hopefully starters, prepare the patient for example, before surgery. This frees the doctor (main course) to perform the actual operation. Follow up care is then undertaken by the dessert, such as physical therapy. Smooth sailing is experienced when all the courses are handled knowingly.

Let's talk about retirement and the choices well suited for the main course. Travel may have been a choice during earlier years of adulthood, but rarely will this course take the baby-boomer years sitting down - literally! Usually the tour group scene is not the first option, although creative ones, such as painting or writing may be enticing. Colorful exotic atmospheres are a good choice. The opportunity to select activities or create their own, are high on the list. Hiking or leisurely strolls, near good food and wine will appeal and likewise be a complement to this course, providing both the appetizer and dessert round out the banquet for them one way or another. Their constitutions tend to be quite strong so they can enjoy it all. This course tends to make their exit embracing all life has to offer!

CHAPTER ELEVEN

Evolution of the Dessert

Let's carry on with our three course meal arriving with the dessert. Now, this course has a rhythm all its own, uniquely different from the appetizer and the main course.

There is a sweetness with delicious lingering energy abiding with the dessert, in fact that is one sure way of identifying this type. Unlike the starter, with its zingy appeal and thirst for more, then the main course possessing a feeling of substance, the dessert is quite simply a delight! Pure enjoyment! Sounds too good to be true? Sometimes we want to hold unto these sensations longer than they are intended for. People who fit this course are meant to be enjoyed at the time for all their splendor, however, depending upon this pleasure for a constant lift can be asking too much. It simply cannot be substantiated, nor was it intended to be. A final wrap up for the other two courses is its perfect role. The traits of the appetizer and the main course are essential for the dessert to balance the meal of the day or life.

How does the dessert experience her/his time in the womb? Gently for the most part, usually causing few waves for the mother. The dessert embraces life with enthusiasm, expecting support, rolling with the ebb and flow of life. The expectant mother can minimize the drama of pregnancy with this course because it may feel "like a piece of cake." The birthing process usually will proceed with little drama.

Now, let's look more closely at the combo of an appetizer mom with this course as her infant. He/she tends to impart a calming effect in the womb, although the need for the substance of the main course is important for the balance of energies. This can be accomplished by the starter mom surrounding herself with main course energy in the form of people or by other means such as strengthening surroundings and food itself. When the mother is a main course, she will do well to have moderate stimulation in her life, mimicking the starter energy again with people and surroundings. Lastly, what if the mother is also a dessert? Lots of bliss! Literally, but be sure to sprinkle with some zest and strength!

What about dad? As we have shared when discussing the other courses - fathers are a great asset in the trio. When he is a starter - he will be a vibrant quality in the meal. If the mom is a starter as well, care must be taken to seek more stability, ensuring the feeling of support to the fetus emotionally. More likely, two starters will not seek each other.

Main course dads have their work cut out for them. Moreover, they generally embrace it with strength and vitality, as can be expected with this course. If the mom is a starter, the balance is a given. If the mom is a main course along with dad, some fun stimuli is the order of the day and the fetus enjoys the ride.

Dessert dads combine energy with the little one in utero, thus mellow energy dominates. When the mom is also a dessert the accompanying energy can be similar to the lingering taste of gelato on the tongue - yummy! Now, the downside is carrying that moment through the day. Not bad - right? But, the need to clear the palate for the next activity may require a little push. Some gentle stimuli just may be the perfect solution.

Speaking of moving on - let's embrace the birth itself. This little one likes a smooth ride, usually the actual emergence will be in accord with this motion. Loving support from the father and others in attendance will be the order of the day. The new mother, regardless of her course should do well. The starter mom may exhibit anxiety, as is her nature, but baring medical complications, should plow through the moment. The main course mom, bringing more strength to the table, will hang in there with her usual tenacity. Sometimes a calming energy is helpful to stay her tendency towards impatience with this seemingly tedious process. The easiest combo between birthing infant and mom is actually dessert with dessert. It may seem like almost too much of a good thing, but it can work beautifully! The only aspect to keep in mind, in this case, is some gently guided physical movement on the part of the laboring mom. The fetus may be somewhat content to not hurry the process. This can be a good thing, but gentle movement can aid the birthing process.

Ahhh! Our little makes a premier appearance! Just as a flaming dessert is brought to the table with pomp and pageantry- so in like fashion is this little dessert. The sweetness of this course must not be confused with the "shrinking violet" image. Usually the dessert is center stage, loving each and every moment! No one is a stranger to this infant, after all who doesn't love a dessert!

The banquet continues to the infancy of our little star and all the delights therein. This shining star typifies the dessert course. In the case of a little girl, she may opt for ballet classes, perhaps even before school age, quickly excelling. Performance is her forte! The only guidance, other than applause, lies in maintaining balance. This course can be highly sensitive (as can the others), but it is less apparent. The remedy for this is for the parent to encourage simple fun activities. Again, I am not in favor of this taking the form of computer games. Recreational activities with family or friends, with little agenda other than ease and laughter are perfect. The fooler with the dessert is the fact he/she plays the starring role, making it appear effortless! This is not the case - actually quite the contrary, much work is put into the act, the same way a luscious dessert looks deceptively easy to prepare. The reality is the fact that it requires a great deal of knowledge and technique to achieve the seemingly effortless result. Another trait of this type is that they overdue. Adequate rest is essential for the mental and physical well being of this course.

When your dessert is a boy, the starring role can look different. I am not limiting the genders to specific roles, just sharing the usual ones.It's true, boys can love and excel in dance, conversely girls in sports. Sports activities will usually grab the passion of the boys. Team sports being the first choice, because of the competitive nature of this course, but the dessert is also a congenial team player.

Childhood and youth will be remembered by much clapping, anxious moments and parental pride! Education is a natural with the dessert, whether standard or alternative academia is the parental choice, this child will more than likely be "the teacher's pet." The act of concentration comes naturally and making high marks is a sought after reward, however, this final course can still pull off being the cheerleader or captain of the team.

Adolescence - the transition time! As with the appetizer and the main course, challenges will present themselves. The biggest surprise is that the ease of parenting this course is sprinkled now with the willfulness of approaching adulthood. Pulling rank, as I like to refer to it, may come into play more significantly now. The dessert is usually a discerning judge of character, however at this time of life the trait may need some parental help. Teens of all types are attracted to the dessert, who has a heart of gold and sometimes extend themselves "where angels fear to tread!" This is a perfect opportunity for mom and dad to take a firm stand to protect their precious dessert of either sex. The word -NO- has a proper use and is important! At the precise moment a behavior of slight rebellion or defiance is exhibited, if the truth be told, gratitude will be felt by the teen for saving face with their peers by saying, "mom and dad won't let me" do whatever the issue seems to be. When single parenting, common today, this stance is even more vital for both parent and child.

Eighteen reigns supreme. In modern culture, this moment signifies maturity, a portal into adulthood. If college is in the immediate picture, there can be some immature times as the dessert vacillates between the peer scene and career preparation. Delegating responsibility to the young adult by he/she assuming financial responsibility, or at least a portion of their educational expense, rather than being carried through by the parents, is the best option. Yes, a part time job, and a full time study can be done! Guess what? It leaves little time for partying and mischief. Is this a hard core attitude? You bet!

Let's view the natural career choices for this type. We have observed that the two previous courses are great openers and organizers, so what's left? Closers! That's right! In the arena of doing business, the dessert is the one who brings the final contract to the board meeting meriting accolades for bringing the project to fruition! In the realm of small businesses, this course completes the job after her/his employees or services have done the groundwork. Professionally, these individuals are perfect for inspecting and putting their seal of approval on work accomplished. Judges are a perfect example. In the medical arena, follow up checks are the work of the dessert, as are the firemen-literally putting out the flame. Disaster crews, bringing relief after the storm are yet another. Let's suppose our dessert is an adventure traveler, their presence may be aiding areas and inhabitants to pick up the pieces of their lives and rebuild their culture.

Let's continue cruising through the life of this final course. Youth may be visibly present well into their older years. If they have paced themselves through their earlier years, taking time to recharge their batteries. Some areas of frustration may be experienced due to the fact they actually do pick up the slack in certain situations. The tendency to be a savior can be present and is actually a deterrent for all concerned. This is the major cause of stress for the dessert. Awareness of the need for individuals to fix themselves is essential in the life journey for this type.

The retirement years can be a delight for the dessert. Remember, they excel in the act of finishing. In actuality, these years will generally be long-lived and succulent in the true essence of this course. What are the natural choices for their "golden years?" Remember when we talked about the inclination of the dessert to be a savior? One of the ways to put this trait to a natural use is being a tour guide. Interesting, no? Think about it - preferably small selected groups, specifically targeted for retirees to travel the globe. It's a bit like a sheep dog and social director all in one! This job fits like a glove with the innate tendencies of this course. It's a win-win for all involved.

There are vast varieties of dessert to choose from in a meal as likewise in our human comparison. The new vogue, although it's been around longer in Europe than in the United States is the airbnb. The bed and breakfast is a more traditional version however, it entails much more work and interaction. This does have an appeal to the dessert for this very reason, especially if one's health and vigor measure up. It is also important to have resources enabling you to hire helpers for this endeavor. The so-called airbnb is easier to pull off, since the guests are left on their own regarding meals and entertainment unless exceptions are made. The drawback to airbnb or similar sites is that more room must be designated, hopefully a private entrance as well as separate kitchens from the main house or owners living space.

With the traditional bed and breakfast only private rooms with a bath are required for each guest or couple. A common living room is usually accessible. The people who choose each of these usually have separate agendas. The airbnb type tend to be more private and independent, while friendly do not feel the need to mingle with the other occupants. The bed and breakfast group are just that groups. They like to feel part of the family in a way and seek out company. They may be trying to escape an unpleasant situation in their personal lives back home or simply very gregarious individuals by nature. Another advantage of the bed and breakfast is the fact more people can be accommodated, but you must enjoy the role of the innkeeper, who literally, in most cases lives with his guests. If the owners have a guest house on the grounds, which they actually occupy, this can be the best of both worlds.

The dessert may also opt for a small getaway in an area of the planet, that affords tranquility with access to camaraderie and fun without any drama. Their finale will be most likely be done with little drama, sweetly peaceful.

CHAPTER TWELVE

THE GLOBAL BANQUET

Speaking of travel - let's take our vision of the three courses worldwide! How do the different cultures fit into our banquet?

We will begin in the good ole USA. Our nation, I believe, is rather unique in its diversity of cultural practices within one country. It's rather, in my opinion, somewhat like several countries squished together. When I travel by car, I often reflect that even without the road signs designating state boundaries, I would recognize the differences in the style of homes.

Moving from east to west, let's get started on our journey. The northeast with it's rugged sea coast attracts a distinct type of individual, for the most part. Guess what? Yes, the appetizer! The rugged individualist, sometimes the fisherman or lobster harvester. Those who gravitate to this area are usually attracted by its drama! Weather is extreme and rather exciting! Seasons of the year are clearly delineated. The cities that are sprinkled throughout this part of the country, retain some of the same characteristics even in the standard businesses. The inhabitants tend to be straight forward and without pretense. These qualities are the very features it's inhabitants find comfortable. One tends to know where they stand. Newcomers need to prove themselves, however once accepted the level of neighborliness is tried and true. How does this echo the appetizer? Consider the clarity and specific qualities of the first course and the sharp distinct tastes they are meant to entice.

Let's continue down the coast to the mid-eastern area. Now, the course changes rather dramatically! We actually see the next course - the main course, arriving before our very eyes! New York and Boston are prime examples of this substantial course, hubs of commerce, meccas for the movers and shakers! People who thrive in these environments are for the most part, decision makers for the major corporations in the country, if not the world. Harvard and other notable centers for learning are also found in this area of the country. The pace is fast, just the ticket for the main course.

Notice how the meal sequence coincides with our journey down the coast. Another similarity with this center area of the northeast is the density of population. Just as the main course is usually the larger portion of the meal, so does this particular area follow suit. The climate of this part of the east is a bit more moderate than its neighbors to the north, however, it too has some highs and lows. But not as extreme.

Soft, gentle climates, reach us as we continue our travels south. The southern regions of the east coast embrace us. What does this sensation remind us of? The dessert of course! The range of different types of desserts match rather well with the differences of the southern states. From the Carolinas, with the lush green mountains truly seeming to be blue, to the red earth of Georgia, then tumbling into our own version of the tropics - Florida. The weather turns to moist and warm, almost smothering in its humidity.

Desserts, too can be overwhelming to our taste buds in large quantities. A little goes a long way is a true statement in this case. What is the general predisposition of the inhabitants of this tasty verdant area? Laid back is the key word! In the early days of colonization of the United States, much of this area was given to large plantations. Fishing was the norm for the more coastal areas of the extreme south. Even the mountains lent themselves to producing food because the winter months were short and the land was fertile. In the tropical areas the growing season was more active in the winter months, when the other parts of the country lay dormant. Farming is still an active industry but, tourism is rampant and perhaps the most sought after commodity. This dessert quality extends itself to complement the other two courses, which it does well!

What speaks of the lusciousness of the dessert more than beaches and soft gentle waves. This brings to mind a crème brûlée or gelato, even more simple a sundae dripping with chocolate syrup. The tropical vegetation also fits this picture most perfectly, palms and beach grass dancing to and fro in the wind.

Progressing on, let's step foot into the Midwest. We will again divide this region into three parts - echoing our meal.

The most northern of this clime encompasses the qualities of the appetizer. Dramatic lakes, ready to display the choppy waves of a rainstorm are nestled in hills or even low mountains. The inhabitants of the Midwest, for the most part, can trace their roots to the Scandinavian part of the world. Immigrants to "the new world " sought the familiar in America. This area is intense in it's weather as well. Strong snowy winters with accompanying temperatures to match embraces a hardy type of population. Of course, modern conveniences, such as central heating, mitigate the need for endurance as once was the case. Agriculture is a mainstay in these states, even though the growing season is relatively short. Cities have sprung up accommodating more diversified people. The beauty of this part of the country during the summer months have brought tourists to spend time, although most of the lake homes are second cottages for city residents.

As we move downward geographically, we come to the heartland of this country. This area is most definitely a main course! The demographics are proof of this characteristic. These people are generally strong, stable, hardworking individuals. The very same people who came this far from the east and decided to remain, not succumbing to the lure of the untamed west years earlier. The terrain also reflects this trait. The elevation is fairly low, without mountains to break the rolling hills. Industry has a strong identity with this region as well, probably due to the strength of its population. The climate is definitely four seasons with each specifically delineated. Humidity accompanies the warm months with moderate to heavy moisture in the form of rain. Snow normally occurs in the winter months. The Great Lakes play a role scenically in this part of the country. Numerous businesses have their bases here, reflecting the stability of this region. A strong Germanic influence is found in evidence in this area's people, as well as other parts of Europe, tracing back to its original settlers.

Traveling down yet further, we embrace the true South - almost another country itself! The cultural traits are quite unique to this region. The eye appeal of this area is accelerated as the flat land turns into rolling hills, then to picturesque mountains making their way down to the sea. Following the same pattern, we experience nature's banquet completing our meal as the perfect desserts.

The people living in these regions, as well, echo these dessert traits. For the most part, a gentility and traditional lifestyle is the order of the day, taking a slightly different spin than the similar course just to the east. The authenticity of this region seems closer to the origins of the people who originally came to tame this wilderness. A sense of separation can be noticed when moving into the true south. The "southern accent" is another clear distinction of this region. Newcomers will be accepted, but it takes a bit of time for the generational families to invite you to their homes. One must earn their trust and acceptance. Conversely, open hearts with a true spirit of community are alive and well here, sometimes more markedly so than other areas of the country. As with the qualities of the dessert, the smooth southern drawl and slow pace add a nice touch to the meal of life.

The extreme southern part gives us perhaps, the only authentic music in America, birthed here, not borrowed from ancestral cultures - the music of New Orleans! A truly varied tray of desserts is presented by this region.

The "Wild West " is coming next in our travels, and wild it still remains in many aspects! Once more, to really appreciate this landscape, we will first embrace the northern states of the west. Strong, jagged mountain peaks make this appetizer landscape quite breathtaking! Heaped with snow in the winter, even remaining on its tips in the summer, creates high drama for the observer. Even the hardy evergreen cannot survive on its highest slopes! The foothills are dotted with cattle, wheat crops and snow fences, in an attempt to keep the roads safe during several months of the year. High fences abound to keep livestock and abundant wildlife away from the motorist as well.

Strong, rugged men and women settled these regions traveling by wagon train to claim these ranch lands. Even today, their descendants occupy ranches handed down by the generations long passed.

A new breed of adventurers are now traveling to this untamed part of America. They are easily identified by the vast array of expensive sports equipment. Shushing down the slopes on skis or snowboards in the winter months, and riding the rivers and skies in the spring and summer. Sports lovers tend to be kind and considerate to this environment since it affords so much pleasure to them. Tourism is a major industry for these mountains. The forests and meadows are havens for hikers and campers when the weather is amiable. The farmers and ranchers usually coexist quite respectfully as well.

Traveling south in this same region, we embrace more rolling grasslands - the foothills. Sunny skies and warmer temperatures embrace us as the main course qualities show themselves. These are the same plains that the buffalo once roamed as far as the eye could see. Ancestral land grants are still in evidence in these regions, retaining some distinct characteristics of this era. The people of this part of the west are a mix of the original native peoples, farmers and nomadic, and the conquerors. Strength and dominance are strongly evidenced in the roots of this land! The solid substance of the main course is strikingly evident in the Southwest! As we near the Gulf of Mexico - the dessert vista makes its presence known. Softer energies come into play, as well as a more gentle appearing quality in the lifestyle of its inhabitants - definitely the dessert.

A new vista awaits us as we travel to the most western part of the United States. The Pacific Northwest is one of the most dramatic landscapes we can encounter!

The ocean and the sea meet in the most intense engaging dance, a spectacle to behold! A tantalizing taste engaging our senses. Giant redwoods, ancient in origin, spread themselves along this terrain. Lumberjacks were among the earliest settlers to this region, attempting to tame the nature here. Now, hopefully the inhabitants behold the strength and care for the nature in this landscape. There remains a sense of independence with a zest for life among the people here, honoring the qualities of the starter in every facet of its being!

Reaching the central part of the west coast, a mellow energy ushers in the main course geographically. The majority of our food is grown in this locality, from grapes for the wine industry, to avocados, nuts, plus a vast assortment of other fruits and vegetables. The temperate climate usually experienced makes a longer growing season than the norm. Steady, industrious individuals populate this area extending inland from the ocean.

Extreme Southern California shifts energetically. The dessert again peeks its head for us. The weather, still warmer, creates more mellow energy.

The waves caressing the beaches are a bit more energetic than the Caribbean, but softer than further north where bathing is usually not possible without a wetsuit. Inhabitants gravitate, in droves, to these southern beaches for their beauty and sunshine. The traffic may not be gentle, but the lifestyle lulls are present here for the luscious dessert qualities to be experienced for those who desire to do so. My next intention is not to explore every continent on the earth, but to give a glimpse of the world as a three course meal.

Asia affords an interesting diversification of cultures and climates. The extreme enormity of the land mass with incredible contrasts sprawls out before us. As we have noticed, the mountainous areas offer grandiose peaks, in actuality the highest in the world! Talk about an appetizer! The colorful specimens of humanity that populate these regions are among the most exotic on the planet! Hardiness beyond belief was required of these inhabitants and only the strongest survived!

As the mountains soften into the plains, again we see the appearance of the main course. Herders and farmers claimed this land with its fertile valleys gracing the landscape. Dipping further south, lush greenery and fragrant blossoms greet our senses. The ocean people with their light clothing, living in homes built near the soft, melodic ocean, sweeps in the dessert course. Reminiscent of a mango sorbet, or flambé, such is the imprint of this tropical paradise!

Venturing slightly westward, we encounter the countries of Eastern Europe. The geographic position of this area of the world has not limited the dramatic role it has played in the scheme of world events, very decidedly the appetizer!

The northernmost regions contain such drastically cold temperatures, it is difficult to even sustain life. Within the portions that make habitation possible, are starters of the most extreme types. This land has seen fierce warrior tribes, many following a nomadic way of life, living with the very herds that sustain them. Even in the present day, the modern lifestyle is not blatantly visible.

Moving southward, the climates again become more temperate as the main course presents itself. Grain and rice fields are visible as are the farmers who sustain these crops. Representing the dedication and fullness of character synonymous with our main course, these people trace their lineage back many generations.

Once more, as we reach the shores of the seas surrounding these sections of the planet, a more gentle population dominates these ancient cultures. The dessert energy of the earth and those who live here, is evident in most cases. Bear in mind, as we navigate our way through this land encompassed by the sea, there are many types of desserts. Some are creamy, slipping along the tongue while others are more spirited, even made flaming by sweet brandy poured over.

Now, moving again in our tantalizing journey,

we embrace the countries of Europe. Northern European countries give us the visual feast of some of the most beautiful mountains in the world- the Alps! What a dramatic starter in our geographical banquet! Not surprisingly, the cultures of this terrain are adventurous, embracing the lifestyle amongst these high elevations with zest and stamina, appetizer style, ready to take on what life has to offer.

The succulent foothills, sloping in the shadow of the high peaks, offer perfect meadows for sheep, goats and cattle to graze. Thus, the main course steps in to captivate our senses with the nourishment these acres offer us. The farms are lovingly tended, often by generations of hard working families, strongly holding these lands. As a main course offers us the strongest nourishment of the meal, these people hold a cultural strength vital to their identity.

The southernmost tip of Europe is indeed its playground! What a splendid dessert displaying all its lusciousness! Long famed for homes of the rich and famous, artists, movie stars - anyone desiring to embrace the sun and warm waters of the Mediterranean! Yes, the joie de vivre, joy of life, is very visible! Those who live here are fun - loving and laid back. Even those who serve the affluent have an attitude of ease, for the most part. Sounds quite delicious, no ?

Now, for Scandinavia and the British Isles. Feeling a little chilled already? The most northerly

Scandinavian countries, surrounded by seas, are truly a splendid example of the appetizer! Sharp, jagged coasts with a high spirited ocean mark the geographic character of this part of the world - a feast for the eyes! Drama also occurs with the climate, some parts of the year having very short days and long colorful nights. The sun does not give a great deal of warmth, with the exception of a few brief months of the year. This region was the birthplace of some of the most hardy sailors- known as the Vikings! Healthy, active individuals call this part of the world home, feasting on the abundant sea life from the waters around them.

Slightly south and west, lie the lands of the British Isles. Surrounded, as well, by the sea, the topography shifts slightly to more tranquil farmlands. Grazing animals dot the grassy meadows, sheep and cattle particularly. Agriculture occupies portions of the land, as well, heralding the main course in our meal. Farming brings the qualities of strength and vitality visibly present in the workers of this land. Larger cities are also within this area, adding a mix of the appetizer and main course depending on the pace and flavor of the city.

The dessert is less present in these climes, except around the gentle coastline villages, which have a soft, delicious sweetness all their own. These small resort hideaways echo a step back in time, with their friendly townsfolk and colloquial lifestyles.

I have only touched the surface describing the

banquet of the world. To me, there is a synchronicity existing in all of nature. Taking this brief word tour, I hope, has given validity to that concept. I find it quite a delicious thought to compare this planet to a grand banquet! There needs to be no reason beyond that!

In the final section of this little manual, I will attempt to show how to have fun with all of these concepts, hopefully making our life's meal a little more palatable, even perhaps delicious!

PART THREE

CHAPTER THIRTEEN

THE DIGESTIF OR AFTER DINNER TOAST

What do we do with all this? Can we actually enhance our quality of life, our relationships with ourselves, then with others, and lastly with the planet? Does it seem overwhelming? There is no need to think of it that way. One of the beautiful awarenesses that has occurred to me was actually the simplicity of it all! Some of you will merely have a good laugh reading all this, then go ahead and have a microwave dinner, what can I say? That's ok, too! If nothing else, at least you found it an entertaining read. Sometime, when you're least expecting it, something may click, as a troublesome person, place or situation arises. On the other hand, please don't feel any of these views are written in stone - they are not!

Try having a three course meal in a specialty restaurant, turn off your cell phone, really relate to your companion or several, as the case may be. You will find a sense of communicating where the only distraction is the party your taste buds are having with such a treat!

An often heard expressed comment today is the lack of fulfillment with it all! What is "it all?" Success in one's profession may leave an unexpected void. Could this be due to the fact that like a poorly balanced meal, it fails to satisfy us? Relationships seem to be in more upheaval than ever, as well. Do we ever ask ourselves how much emotional time, soul time, we truly invest in relating to the other person? I am not suggesting that having a lovely satisfying meal with this person will iron out all the wrinkles, actually the opposite may happen! You may come to the realization upon this experience, you have little or nothing in common. The benefit of this experience is precisely that you allowed yourself to check out this meal in depth without distractions! Just as in trying the different tastes comprising your banquet, you have discovered true enjoyment or experience distaste, but, you did give it a go!

Now, the upside is that it happens, for most of us, we find to our surprise a new and exotic meal with well - coordinated courses really turns us on! The exact similar chain of events can occur when encountering strange and different people and places. I am not suggesting we betray our natural instincts regarding these things, quite the contrary, but take that leap! Think about success stories of those who left their comfort zone. All we are really talking about here is food, but the parallel can be made by taking it further.

Those of us who tend to grab onto a new theory, or suggested truism, and turn it into a hard core discipline is not what I intend in any way! Embracing life as a luscious banquet is meant to illustrate the importance of living in joy! I cannot equate sadness, misery and lack as anything beneficial for humanity! One of the reasons I used world geography is to show how nature celebrates its own meal, balanced and nourishing!

I believe the reason we were given such a beautiful planet to live on is precisely to enjoy ourselves! Belief systems have arisen creating negative premises involving pleasure. We do not live in a black and white world! We are surrounded by luscious, colorful, fruits and vegetables to sustain our bodies! Why limit ourselves? It is said, a true gourmet needs only a few succulent spoonfuls to satisfy his soul, therefore, I am not advocating misuse of nature's gifts. Quite the contrary, conscious eating and drinking are the only way to truly enjoy our meals. I do acknowledge, some foods or drinks are not appropriate for certain individuals, however, the choices are so vast we can navigate around those and choose alternative selections.

Time is of the essence to enable us to enjoy life in general. This is another parallel to the three courses. The course selections can be small and truly savored. Have you ever taken the time to truly savor each and every moment? Time, literally, will feel as if it has stood still! Once more, using the banquet illustration, the secret to truly enjoying a fabulous meal is devoting time to engage your taste buds with each and every mouthful! Just as the secret to truly living life is to experience each and every moment in every essence of your being! Rushing through life is similar to wolfing down a meal-indigestion! Too much, too fast with no lasting satisfaction!

Let's sum up all this by thoughts of embracing "the meal of our lives" with awareness of the types of choices our courses present us with. The wonderful balance the sequence of these courses give to us in the form of the people in our lives, the activities, places, even climates to enable us to be better human beings leading more fulfilling lives! Yes, and eat better, too!

QUESTIONS AND ANSWERS

I am including this section to hopefully answer some anticipated questions you may have. I am also available for workshops and consultations to take this further in an even more personal way.

Perhaps the first question we all have is "how can I know what course I am?" Can I be a combination? Lastly, does my course type change during my lifetime? So, how can we really figure out which part of the meal we actually are? It's really quite easy. We have given an overview earlier, but let's get even more specific.

Appetizers are, of course, where we begin. Let's ask ourselves- just how do we go at life? I used the term "go at life" for a special reason. Appetizers approach life much like a race car driver gets ready for the track, with a great deal of zest, vigor and spontaneity! There is preparation, but done with relentless energy. Do you seem to go nonstop during your day? Do you feel overwhelmed and in desperate need of help, only to find it doesn't meet your satisfaction? These are all signs of the starter per-sonality. Remember, I said all courses are necessary and delightful, but there is the necessity to balance each one and help is needed to decipher the special qualities.Varying degrees of this check list, as with the vast array of appetizers available for a meal, can challenge us a bit in making our decision. A word of caution, sometimes starters feel there is something faulty associated with the role of the appetizer. Nothing could be further from the truth! These traits are a WOW to life, as are the important begin-nings to a meal, setting the tempo for the following courses. Balance is the key to keeping the appetizer personality on an even keel with life. Now, that we have spelled out quite specifically the life traits of the starter, we will give some suggestions to enable us to truly enjoy them. Before we get into all of that, let's get into the main course.

In some European countries, this course is re-ferred to as "the plat." This simply means the sub-stantial part of the meal. How can we recognize the main course or "plat" characteristics in ourselves? Right off the bat - we think we can do it all! Now, compared to the appetizer, who usually recognizes the need for team work, the main course tries to take it all on singlehanded. Sound familiar? It's a bit tricky because sometimes a dessert can mask as a main course, but in the long run the "plat" people have a different kind of stamina. This course - the main course exhibits a strong endurance but, does well to know its limits. The starter relies on this stamina, just as the main course should appreciate the starter. Then the "plat" (main course) comes in on cue to move everything along and carry the weight of the moment that has gotten off to a good start. Another word of caution for this course personality is to realize they can graciously acquiesce to the dessert bringing a smooth conclusion.

I know what is going through your mind. "While all this is well and good, how do we live life without a trio at our fingertips?" I shall cover this question just a little later as we discuss how to put these principles into action, quite specifically, in our day to day life.

Another trait of the main course is the tendency to appear like a "Lone Ranger" but, this can be deceptive because actually this type usually desires the company of others. Sometimes shyness makes the main course reticent to reach out to others.
People will often see this person as always having it all together, when in reality they are working very hard, though not wanting to look like it. When we use our three course meal as a comparison, upon analyzation, the gourmet knows the appetizer readies the palate for the main course, stimulating it, either subtly or dramatically! Enter the main course, sometimes viewed as the star of the meal, but in actuality is just performing its role. The curtain call - the dessert brings a dramatic or sweet finish - sometimes both!

Now, let's explore the dessert people. These traits are sometimes difficult to pin down, but hopefully we will clarify them for you. To begin with dessert beings are sweet! I know that sounds like an old cliche, but in this situation it is spot on. Desserts are easy to order and hard to resist. The yummy choices can complicate the issue, but desserts are fun, right? If you possibly think you might be a dessert, here are a few questions to ask yourself. Do you find yourself the one who usually pulls everything together? Are you the savior type? Do people gravitate to you easily and want to keep you in their circle of friends? If the answer to these questions is yes, there is a strong chance you are indeed a dessert! Now, as with all courses, there is a need for balance and the same rule of thumb holds true here. When, or if this course tries to be"a one man band," it can fall short. What I mean is that the dessert in a meal is meant to follow - first the appetizer, then the main course and be the grand finale! This finale was NOT intended to be a meal in and of itself! If this is attempted, instead of a sensation of pleasure, a feeling of lack of satisfaction ensues. The same principle can be successfully applied to people who identify with being desserts. When these individuals attempt "to do it all" they run the risk of energy burnout, but because of their giving nature are not conscious of this fact! There is a saying "two is company, three is a crowd." In the interest of this way of looking at things that can be erroneous! Let's take the example of three people going out to dinner together. One is an appetizer, one is a main course, and one is a dessert. It has been my personal experience this can be the perfect trio. Why? Because, quite simply each plays their part and as they say the rest is only history, but a great meal!

As we shared briefly, earlier in the manual, there are ways and means we can incorporate into life's situations to create this balance, even when not in the form of physical players. Please, do not think I am telling you not to have those romantic dinners for two, or with a good friend, or even solo if the plan arises. I will show how subtle choices in the environment can pick up any energetic slack - no problem whatever!

Next question - can I be a combination of more than one course? Using my theory - I say no. Of course, these are only guidelines, you are free to think as you choose. When I decide upon my own course traits, and those of others, the boundaries are quite clear. Perhaps this is a time to remember that there are an extremely large range of foods within each course selection. Likewise, personalities can vary widely, still retaining their specific similarities to a respective course. The simplicity and beauty of this logic lies in keeping the three courses distinct!

The third question I would like to address is whether we change courses throughout our lifetime? Again, keeping to this basic thought pattern - I say no. I do repeat, however, the variety of foods in each category offer much diversification when considering personality types.

Before we go into detail regarding our lifestyles

within each respective course, I would like to address our eating habits. You probably enjoy food or you would not have been attracted to this book, however, a little food can go a long way. In other words, perhaps we do not want a three course meal in one sitting, so how can this work? Easily, actually, in one of several ways. One choice is to incorporate each course in a single plate offering. By this, I mean having a small serving of an appetizer food accompanying the main course on the plate. Ideally, one should eat the respective courses sequentially, not together, but it works either way. Dessert for the one dish method can be simply a piece of exquisite chocolate or waiting a short time to enjoy your final course. The second, more gourmet approach, is to present tiny servings course by course. Michelin, and other fine restaurants use this approach. Lastly, for dieters, think of the intake of foods over the entire day as your three course meal . This is a slightly unorthodox approach, but it is actually quite effective health wise, yet satisfying for the taste buds, while providing the desired balance.

Relationships in depth - Course by Course
How does this work

Beginning with the starter as always, let's look closely how the appetizer energy works in relationships. Starters usually have little difficulty attracting a partner or friends. Their zest and energy adds spice to life by being very enticing, just as an appetizer does in a meal. Now, let's cruise through all the possible combinations that may occur. First, and foremost are those individuals who are energetically attracted verses those who just seem to end up together in the path of life. Starters are generally not a magnet for each other - too much zing one could say. But, what happens when these identical types are in each other's company? First off, let's hope they are very different types of appetizers. Yes, that does exist and makes life easier in this case. Another part of the picture is the specific atmosphere this interaction plays out in. Sometimes it seems simply fate, but if choices are available- relaxed non stimulating surroundings are very helpful, somewhat mimicking the main course. This energetically calms the intensity of the double starters.

The addition of dessert aspects really rounds it out. This can take the appearance of a gentle completion of the event. This double appetizer attraction is almost always a dead end when it comes to a romantic relationship. I can hear the question- oh - what should I do? I am already married or committed to a starter, and I think I am one too. First, don't panic! Apparently, unless you are miserable and looking for a way out, you must be doing something right. Quite possibly, neither of you are extreme forms of this course. For example, how about soup and salad? One is a little crisp and refreshing, while the other is soothing and rich. You see some appetizers almost fit the main course category, this is also true of people. Some awareness can be given to completion as that is the arena of the dessert. Remember, the more substantial appetizer is simulating the main course, picking up the slack if you will, but the completion role of the dessert is missing. Organizing one's schedule to encourage completion of tasks could be just the way to accomplish this.

Now, let's look at a more common combo - the appetizer and the main course. This duo more often occurs when choosing your significant partner or a good friend. There are some qualities, however, that bear looking at. Starters generally gravitate to the main course types with the main course joining in. Why? The reason this sequence occurs is that the starter needs the main course energetically more than the main course is dependent on the starter. I know in this day and age the word "need" is frowned upon as taboo energetically in relationships. But, seriously if there were no "needs" out there for mankind, we would be quite happy as loners and I sincerely believe this is not true! We are actually somewhat tribal by nature, but that is another story. Pursuing this theory is the reason that the grounding, nutritive aspects of the "plat" or main course is a necessary energy for the starter. The "plat," being a bit more of a stronger presentation, is less aware of the enhancement that can be experienced by the appetizer. However, once the connection has been established these two can really hit it off. The only missing component, then becomes the dessert. Planning one's lifestyle to achieve goals in a relaxed fashion covers this base quite nicely.

Lastly, in the personal relationship arena for the starter - enter the dessert. Believe it or not, this is the most common attraction. Why? Opposites attract and it is usually mutual, but there are pitfalls to be avoided. Starting off, the appetizer is an instant draw for the dessert because of the stimulation. This is the characteristic trait of the starter, whereas the final course traits are smooth, delectable and easy going. You may ask, wherein lie any problems? Well, we are missing the strength of the meal in the guise of the main course. Why does that matter, is the next question? It's rather like starting the meal and finishing the meal with no real sense of fulfillment, which is precisely the purpose of the plat or main course. So, how does this play out?

One possible scenario is a sense of lack experienced by each person. Ok, so how do we fix this, simply by incorporating meaningful experiences of substance in our lives. Literally, having a quiet, nourishing meal together, not just a snack or fast food. A full bodied entertainment, such as a concert, play, ballet, or even a movie (if it has depth and meaning) could suffice. Get my point? Frivolous, flippant entertainment does not fill this need. While we are on the subject of "a night out" amusement parks and loud concerts definitely do not belong in this category. They have their place, but do not provide the energetic balance between the two courses. There is also the distinct possibility that the main course type person would make up the bulk of their circle of friends, a natural oc-currence. It's fine to trust fate, but I also believe in giving it a helping hand. By all means don't become upset, nor give undue concern, just relax and reflect, perhaps putting into use a clue or two presented here.

Now - The Main Course

Main courses may think they have it nailed be-cause of their strength and purposefulness. Sorry to say- not true! This is not to say they do not have a lot going for them (as all courses have in their own way) but, plats do well to remember they are a course in the meal - not the whole banquet. We have cruised through the combo of the main course and the appetizer, but with our focus on the appetizer. Now, we will look at this duo from the point of view of the plat (main course.)

Main courses are a natural in the field of attrac-tion when it comes to starters. Actually the starters may kick off the action, as is natural for them, but the main course will more than likely respond read-ily. Just as in a meal, the appetizer preceded the principle course, but the main course is ready and waiting. Why? The main course likes to be in the spotlight, both personally and in the banquet. The drama of the starter is the perfect foil for the plat to bask in! How does this work in one to one involve-ment? At first, it's a match made in heaven, but remember there is a reason for the applause of the dessert. Translated into human interactions we find there can be too much expectation placed upon the personality of the main course from the appetizer energy. The main course likes to carry the show, but in reality there can be a sense of drain if this is experienced on a regular basis. Obviously, hanging out with dessert types, whenever possible, distributes the energetics beneficially for both the starter and the main course.

On a daily basis, rather than being concerned with a trio of physical beings, there are activities that can provide a similar balance. The main course would be wise to engage in undertakings that provide a soothing, refreshing sense of well being. These can be done with the starter partner to give a dessert type of energetic balance to the lifestyle.

Now, when two main courses get together, it can really get interesting. This is actually a frequent happening, believe it or not, it is definitely a situation of like attracts like. The good times are usually very good, but the turbulent times, very rough! Why? Too much energy, plain and simple - too heavy and too strong! What's the solution? Lighten up! In this case, activities that are exciting and dramatic can be just the ticket, mixed with a nice smooth finish! Incorporating such activities in your lifestyle, in this situation, really works.

Lastly, discussing the main course and pairings, let's carry on with the main course and dessert. Main courses, generally speaking love this combo! Why? The principle course still holds center stage and the dessert is usually just fine with this state of affairs. Is there a downside? Well, a bit of boredom may occur for the main course. The sweetness, literally may wear thin at times. What to do? Spice it up! Have those uproarious friends over for an evening, even though you can't handle them too often. Competitive sports, either personally participated in, if it's your thing, or vicariously watched, or even competitive board games can be quite stimulating, if there's a need. I do not include video games in this suggestion due to the fact they are more geared to solo playing.

Now, the final course - the dessert! Let's begin with the pairing of the appetizer and dessert. Is it a usual happening? Somewhat surprising, yes it is! We spoke of it previously, from the starters side of the coin, now let's flip the coin and view it from the dessert side of the menu. This course tends to take it slow and easy. It's their virtue and their vice from the appetizer's point of view. They are more likely to accept the advance, not initiate it. This can occur even on a friendship level, which brings me to share the fact that even in a romantic attraction, it may be difficult to discern the dessert's motive. This is sometimes most disconcerting to the starters out there. Pressure and manipulation usually are not helpful in the least. The final course type will take his or her sweet (literally) time to make the objective clear. This shows itself even in social settings based on a strictly platonic level. Decisions on joining a gathering or basically committing to an event, can cause frustration, particularly for the appetizer. The solution lies in the energy of incorporating main course energy into the mix. If the situation is a one on one, then engaging in a set schedule helps to alleviate some of the indecisiveness common for the dessert. An engaging lifestyle adding more substance to the normal activities can also mimic the missing main course energy.

Desserts are very palatable and adapt enjoyably to the appetizer. Once more from their point of view, they really gravitate to the energetic starters. The only caution is too much of a good thing - such as never ending get up and go, evidenced by some appetizers. Temporary burnout can be felt by the dessert in such cases. The saving grace is moderation, which is the quality of the main course. If this burnout is evident, the starter should back off and engage in less intense activities. This helps to add the main course stabilizing energy to balance the situation. One need not worry over these happenings, just realize if the energies seem a little stressed, try to interject one or more of the above suggestions.

The dessert and main course are interesting from the eyes of the dessert. This can seem like a match made in heaven and for the most part it is. The strength of the main course is very much appreciated by the dessert. Desserts are usually delighted to bring up the rear and closing act. This is the delight of the main course, thus the experience of compatibility. The dessert does not desire to play center stage, being quite happy in its position as the finale. So, what could possibly be a bump in the road? Lack of fireworks! Isn't that what the appetizer does well in a larger or smaller way? When that issue comes up, just add a little spice to the mix. This can be done in the form of a person who fits the role of a starter, or an activity that does the same job. We have already mentioned some, but to recap, anything that is a bit exciting or stimulating should do the trick. When the main course is spirited along a bit with it's full bodied nourishment, it sometimes is all that is needed.

Dessert and dessert form an unusual, but not impossible twosome, both in intimate relationships, or simply the realm of friendship. Talk about mellow - you've got it with this pairing! Again, if the desserts are vastly different the energetics vary. In addition, some desserts just simply go together, enhancing each other. Think pie or cake with ice cream, or a creamy dessert with luscious whip cream! Mouthwatering, right? Now think about how long the satisfaction of this combo would last without any other courses of the meal. You are getting the picture.

So, once again, we simply add to the mix - quite easily actually. Let's take the subject, once again, of the members of our social circle. When it's appropriate, invite that person who is definitely a "live wire" - perfect appetizer energy. Remember that interesting friend or acquaintance that always provides some humorous stories of nourishing wit or sustainable information? Bring these personalities together! No need to do this with great frequency if it doesn't flow. I do guarantee the energy will create a balanced experience, at least from time to time.

Now, on a daily basis, let's reflect the ways we can choose to spend our time together. This could be the case when that wild music venue is just the thing to liven up the scene. When dining out, select foods that are a bit of a trip on the wild side for the taste buds. Make sure you include the appetizer and main course, soft pedaling on the dessert, as that course is well taken care of by the two respective personalities present. The daily life for the dessert can, on the whole, be literally "a piece of cake." Stop all undue concern, but also embrace your adventurous side with the remaining courses as well.

One consideration that comes to mind is the situation of the single man or woman. We have all experienced this time in lives, either as a interim between relationships, or a path through life. It's important to be able to apply these theories to this time. We have touched on all the combos and trios, now let's consider me, myself and I.

Beginning as always with the appetizer, let's view the solitary existence. Starters are generally very gregarious by nature, but they can burn through acquaintances rather quickly without knowing what went wrong. Our purpose is not to discuss attracting other people in our lives, we all do that, but the alone times we face. How do we deal effectively with these moments? To begin with, let's look at the atmosphere surrounding the appetizer. Is it cluttered and in chaos? Not the way to go for this course. They tend to be flitting around a mile a minute as it is. The last thing they need is to have disorder in their environment. Now, this seeming disorganization may not appear that way to the starter, so it's vitally important to take a somewhat critical look at the space you live in.

It's very true, the appetizer gets a lot done, but scheduling needs to have time allotted for clean-up and organization as well as down time. This may not be a priority to the appetizer. Here is the need for the energy of the main course coming through daily life - discipline! This trait may not come naturally to the starter. Remember their purpose is to ignite the taste buds. If we are a solo act, we better get it together by organizing our space to ground our energy, much as a main course does with a meal. Dessert comes to us when we complete what we start. Appetizers are great initiators, but left to their own devices may lack the motivation to finish a project, even if it's to clean the house. Incorporating these modes of operation into your pattern of living will balance the starter nicely.

There is another point worth considering - that is physical eating patterns. Starters tend to eat quite lightly (there are exceptions) yet, it is important that main course type foods are included, even in small quantities, in this diet for solidifying energy. A smooth dessert, even if only one bite, is a good finish to complete the appetizer's meal. Remember I shared thinking of spreading our three course meal over the space of a day if desired, rather than feel it must be enjoyed in one sitting.

Let's move our courses right along to the main one. It is quite interesting to observe the eating habits of this course on a singular basis. The plat (as I sometimes refer to it) appears to enjoy the time alone, however looks can be deceiving! The main course seems to have self-sufficiency nailed! Not quite true. They stand alone fairly well, but the absence of the appetizer and dessert energy can rear its head in unusual ways. First, the main course may experience loneliness, as the others can too, but with the plat it is usually hidden. Friends often call on this type when they need them, but rarely stop to consider the main course's needs because they usually don't let them show. Another aspect of this course is that it's vital for them to be recognized and needed. In the perfect scheme of things, they would be sandwiched in between the first and last course, this center stage is a lifeline for the main course. So how is this accomplished solo? Be open to reorganizing this situation, if you resonate with it. Look at your environment. Is it stimulating and at the same time warm and cozy? It's rare that minimalism works for this course.

Obviously, confiding wisely with a trusted friend or two, is a good move. It's not ok to carry the whole meal, if you get my point. Be considerate of yourself and treat yourself well! Main courses can be very critical, sometimes cutting themselves little slack. Remember, you are part of the meal - yes - a vital one, but it's not all about you!

Eating practices can fill a gap here too. Have a little starter to get the meal going, with a sweet treat to finish. Once more, it's not about the amount, but the significance of the balance. Main courses are usually hard workers, observe this and take time for fun. This can come in the form of sports - not necessarily hard core, but with some stimulation and challenge. Walks or hiking fit well for the main course, they can be as gentle or exciting as you like. Swimming is also a good choice, it takes the sparkle of the starter and the gentle finish of the dessert into your moments.

Lastly, but not least by any means is our dessert. What would life be like without the sweet reward this course brings to our life? As you have guessed by this time, my philosophy is to embrace the joys of life responsibly, yet fully! This finale for the meal is quite an intricate package, if you will. My meaning lies in the fact that the dessert type is a "let's get the job done and done well!"

How does that translate for the single person embodying these characteristics? Rather a big responsibility, wouldn't you say? Desserts come in many guises with a wide variety of traits, overall there is graciousness present. There is also a bit of a tendency to play the savior. Have you ever had a mediocre meal, then finish with a fabulous dessert? It's the end you remember! It's the yummy taste that lingers. One tends to forget the preceding food that didn't quite impress you. Yes, the dessert takes that role rather seriously! While keeping it under wraps the "happy ending" responsibility can weigh heavily on the dessert type when doing a solo act. The other courses, appetizer and main, can take a load off for this individual.

There are ways to bring stimulation and endurance into their daily lives. Desserts can become "rutty." By this , I mean there can be a tendency to boredom by allowing daily routine to lack spontaneity. The energy of the starter can be brought into everyday activities by purposefully doing so. How? You may ask? Observe your activities over a week, check for lack of variance. Check your meals. Do they have some zing and substance, or are too many snacks making up for real dining. Dessert types can also be addicted to fast food eating - not in their best interests! I feel final courses need to take appropriate time for themselves by indulging in balanced, delicious meals. These should be thoughtfully prepared, instead of always rushing to FINISH the next task! Free time is well spent involving oneself in activities that are varied, both energizing and fulfilling!

Desserts can also take the other end of the spectrum. They may tend toward being "couch potatoes" spending too much time in front of the screen, computer or tv and snacking. Get up! Add the vigor of the starter and sustainability of the main course. Balance is easily recognized when a sense of well - being is felt, making life enjoyable!

The Final Area Of Exploration
Travel and Vacation Moments

The final area of exploration in The Banquet of Our Lives is travel and vacation moments, where to go, what to see and do! Wildly enough, using these ideas regarding meal types can be a great help choosing fun trips, or even places to live, long or short term.

We have touched on this subject earlier, but I would like to elaborate more extensively. Most people agree traveling together can be stressful. We may think we know a friend, then when we experience traveling with them, we find we are totally mistaken. Romantic relationships can end abruptly after the long awaited trip together! Why? Hopefully, I can shed a little light on this situation. There are actually several reasons this happens using this thought system to explain.

Right off the bat, as they say, just because we have had a few good times together, in the case of friends, does little to ensure we can endure the varied experiences of travel and still tolerate each other. Let's look at the actual time and circumstances we have experienced in this person's presence. How long, a frequent evening or weekend? Have we been in a group setting or one on one? Most of the time, if we examine these encounters closely, we will notice that usually there have been others present, in addition to specific events distracting intense personal interaction. That is why tours have such popularity. It mimics most types of social interaction and is less stressful than individual travel in some ways. The other plus, some may encounter, in group travel is a specific dedicated focus. These can be as varied as art classes, writing classes or cooking classes, as well as different sports oriented activities. If this mode of travel sounds appealing to you, there are a few questions to ask yourself.

Are you traveling solo? If so, what course type do you think you are, at this point nail it! Do you gravitate to an active event filled schedule, or a more leisurely pace? Is covering lots of ground in your sightseeing agenda or spending quality time in select places? Apply the previous info regarding leisure time and see what fits.

As a quick recap - appetizers need more mellow, nourishing selections. A word of caution, sometimes we may resist the very balance we need and gravitate toward the familiar. In the case of the starter, that translates to mean a very busy activity a minute vacation. What is likely to happen is burnout! It is important though, that some stimulation is included or boredom will ensue. The opposite is true for the main course people, a little zing is a good thing!

Main courses tend to like scheduling agendas, but a surprise to two adds the needed spice. Desserts need the stimuli and the planning, or they may just lie on the beach all day. But, you may say - I don't like group travel - what then? If you are truly a solo traveler being gregarious is a must! I would also advise against more than a couple weeks at a time, unless you have contact people along the way. When traveling alone more street smarts and homework around your accommodations are vital! Using our course guidelines, make your choices accordingly to balance your energies regarding places to visit and anticipated activities. It's fine to leave time for adventure, but using discretion. Winging it, leaves much to be desired when traveling by one-self!

If the choice is to travel with a tried and true friend, or better yet a lover, once more use the guidelines we have shared. Be clear in determining your type and the other person's type. What energies must be added to create the full meal, thus emotional nourishment? Actual eating preferences and needs must be carefully addressed. Personal choices regarding leisure time (where no specific activities distract) are key to creating a pleasurable holiday. We may feel we know a person well, but as the saying goes, you never really know anyone until you live with them. Even in the case of someone we do, in fact live with, our life at home is vastly different than the stresses of even a well planned vacation. Thinking in terms of course types gives us clues in this arena. For example, appetizers, as previously stated, are highly energetic. What's more, they need to have an outlet for that energy. Main course types are rather moderate in this arena, and desserts can be even lethargic. Again the key is balance!

Now, is a good time to refer back to the geographic description of our banquet and the places on the planet that carry certain types of these energies.

Ah! The appetizer! This course is usually quiet sporty by nature, consequently a get away filled with activity will usually top the list. The important consideration, however, needs to be time to chill. Downtime is an absolute must for the starter! If two starters team up - wow the energetics could be a bit overwhelming! Cycling, climbing, rafting, intense hiking are just a few choices that immediately appeal to these courses. The places on the planet best suited to these sports are also appetizer type terrains. Now, the saving grace is that hopefully the starter or starters are in the company of a main course type and or a dessert. This would be a tremendous help. These other two courses actually benefit more from the stimulation of the above scenario. They approach the activities with a little less intensity, maybe even encourage relaxing interludes in the mix. Get the picture? Just as a meal flows when the taste buds are not overwhelmed with one course, so do related personalities move more slowly when energetic needs are met. When a locale is selected by the starter that is predominantly main course or dessert course energy dominate - some exciting activities can be introduced. A perfect illustration of this would be a tropical getaway on a lovely beach. Pretty laid back for the appetizer person, but scuba diving or even sport fishing livens up the screen.

Let's spend a moment to consider the main course as a traveler. This individual is the perfect organizer. Every detail researched and evaluated well in advance of the planned trip. Amazingly enough, travel in and of itself, has a way of setting a bit astray the best laid plans. This actually works in favor of the "plat" or main course. It adds a bit of spice to the experience, just as a starter adds a zing to get the meal underway.

This course normally chooses a moderately active time of it, sightseeing, long walks in the village or countryside - even cities with comfortable accommodations. Yes, moderation, but not boring. The place this course may choose might be hilly, lush areas with interesting architecture and exotic culture. Travel is seldom so comfortable that it lacks excitement, which is important for this course. Cruises may not prove to be the best choice, unless some stimulating places are visited along the way.

The dessert is usually a delightful traveler for those in his or her company, but how is it for the dessert? Are their needs being met and energies balanced in the total scheme of the journey? What kind of atmosphere works best for this course? Remember, we mentioned the dessert sometimes takes on the savior role, just as the final course can save the day for the meal. But, one may ask, what are the specific needs of this personality type? Well, stimulation and stamina, just the attributes the previous courses in an actual meal provide - hopefully. Another role the dessert may play out in the world, travel or home, is that of a peacemaker- saving the situation. This is another aspect of the savior role. In group scenarios, this may take the form of acquiescing ones real needs for the sake of the group, or even the other person in a duo scene.

The final course must be clear regarding their own needs, perhaps not always expecting these to be met, but feeling strong enough to assert oneself when possible and practical. Seeking choices that enhance their own balance is vital to the wellbeing of this course. Choices of destinations and activities, when planning that get - away trip, must be looked at with this in mind for their own enjoyment. The planned agenda can include some wild, exciting happenings, as well as full - bodied times to unwind. Extreme sports may not fit this type generally, but certainly physical activities, particularly to indulge in special interests, such as hiking, museums and other scenic marvels. Geographically many atmospheres are suitable. Mountains, meadows, and even beaches are great possibilities. Large metropolitan cities can work, especially those with lovely sections for a stroll, but perhaps less obvious choices for the dessert type.

Lastly, how about the home bodies who are not world travelers? What's a way for them to recharge? How about a short weekend getaway? Perhaps just a day's drive, maybe only hours away from home? Most areas of the world have scenic wonders within easy reach, perhaps not overly dramatic, but nonetheless charming. The same guidelines apply to these mini trips. Bear in mind the missing courses of the participants and simply fill in the gaps. Be creative, search out elements that bring the other energies within our range of experience.

The most important element in any banquet is the sensation of fulfillment! This, I believe parallels life itself! My purpose in sharing this little book with you is simply to be a bit of a guide to accomplish that goal! Life should be stimulating, nourishing, and sweet! Does it get any better than that? Enjoy The Banquet of Our Lives! Bon appétit!

ABOUT THE AUTHOR

Raynera Mrotek

I want to express my love
and devotion to my fam-
ily! These loved ones have
given me so much inspir-
ation for my book. I also
want to acknowledge the 
incredible people who have crossed my path, pro-
viding me the insights to share with you my readers.
As you may have guessed, I have a great passion for
what makes people tick. I have studied psychology,
but I am not a therapist. My way of comparing personalities to food courses evolved from my life's
work with people. Delicious, exquisitely prepared
food is a love of mine, my concepts were born from
that enjoyment!

I am available for workshops and consultations.

Visit my website www.themealofourlives.com for
details.

ACKNOWLEDGEMENT

I want to acknowledge my son Andrzej for his tireless expertise in editing, formatting and giving "The Meal Of Our Lives" the final touches for publishing.

www.ingramcontent.com/pod-product-compliance
Lightning Source LLC
Chambersburg PA
CBHW020549160726
47991CB00002B/657